PRAISE FOR *THE WANDERING RADIANCE*

"Hilde Domin wrenched from the darkest of times a formidable belief in the radiance that nonetheless exists in life. Mark S. Burrows' exceptional translation brings that radiance into our present. This is a collection for all with a stubborn faith in humankind's powers of survival—and transcendence."
  —Stephanie Dowrick, author of *In The Company of Rilke*

"These shimmering poems by Hilde Domin lodge in the heart and blaze in the mind as they trace the journey of a deep soul through exile and self-realization. I would recommend these vivid poems to anyone who cares about the transformative power of great poetry."
  —Jay Parini, author of *New and Collected Poems: 1975-2015*

"'into the dark place / at the end of memory': this is the journey on which Hilde Domin takes the reader in this delicate and sensitive translation by Mark S. Burrows, the first full-length collection of the German poet's work in English. Loss and exile, voyaging out and returning, our transience upon the face of the earth, the way we are bound to ourselves and the world through love—Hilde Domin treats these themes with the gentlest of touch and the greatest of seriousness. Burrows has rendered her deceptively simple language into an English that is as translucent as the original, letting Domin's poetic spirit shine through, 'Freed / a word does its work / on the water of time /…This word from me to you, / this drifting leaf…' We have here a fitting introduction to this major postwar German poet."
  —Hilary Davies, author of *Exile and the Kingdom*

"For years we shared Hilde Domin's poems photocopied from anthologies, eager for each of her blazing suns, our favorite forecast! We tired of the lukewarm men of her generation translated again and again, but we believed the crimes of publishing would eventually be set right. Here is the book we have been waiting to carry into the day; oh, how we have been waiting!"
  —CAConrad, author of *While Standing in Line for Death*

D1562332

"These poems by the German Jew Hilde Domin, presented in the original and in English translation, speak of her complex experience of 'exile and homeland', experience which taught her—in the words of the short essay so aptly chosen to introduce the collection—that language, the mother-tongue of her childhood, is 'the last irrevocable home'. It was for this language that Domin eventually returned to Germany after twenty-two years of wandering. In other languages than German, says Domin, she remains forever a guest. How fitting and moving, then, that in *The Wandering Radiance*, her poems should be 'hosted' in the simplicity and clarity of this translation! In Mark S. Burrows' English words, Domin evokes not only her own experience, but the existential loneliness that is common to all; and there is solace in the recognition that this loneliness is paradoxically shared."
    —Jean Ward, Head of Literary Studies in English, University of Gdańsk

"*The Wandering Radiance* invites readers to become acquainted with Hilde Domin's journey between homeland and exile. Mark S. Burrows' impressive translation of her poems conveys their moving and freeing power. These are texts whose depths and beauty Domin herself arrived at through her lifelong work as a translator, an engagement that honed her ability to draw upon the dynamism of words in creating poetic images with a distinctive style. Burrows has succeeded in carrying the radiant power of her poems over to the shoreline of his native tongue. This is an enrichment for all who long to be stirred by the courage and resilience she embodied as a Jewish writer who said of herself, upon returning to Germany following decades in exile: 'I stepped into the air, and it carried me.'"
    —Vera-Sabine Winkler, author of *Leise Bekenntnisse. Die Bedeutung der Poesie für die Sprache der Liturgie am Beispiel von Hilde Domin*

"'The loss of the sense of belonging,' Hilde Domin writes in her essay 'Exile and Homeland,' which prefaces this celebration of her work, 'is a wounding that never scars entirely.' Perhaps the act of writing might not heal either author or reader, but Domin shows us what radiance is possible while living in 'permanent flight.' She is an essential poet for our current time and for those to come."
    —Rosebud Ben-Oni, author of *If This Is the Age We End Discovery*, Finalist for the 2021 National Jewish Book Award in Poetry

The Wandering Radiance

Selected Poems of
Hilde Domin

The Wandering Radiance

Selected Poems of
Hilde Domin

Translated and Introduced
by Mark S. Burrows

Foreword by Marion Tauschwitz

BILINGUAL EDITION

Green Linden Press

GREEN LINDEN PRESS
208 Broad Street South
Grinnell, Iowa 50112
www.greenlindenpress.com

ISBN: 978-1-7371625-6-8

First printing, 2023

Library of Congress Cataloging-in-Publication Data

Names: Domin, Hilde, author. | Burrows, Mark S., 1955– translator.
Title: The Wandering Radiance : selected poems / Hilde Domin
Identifiers: LCCN 2022046877 | ISBN 9781737162568 (paperback)
Subjects: LCGFT: Poetry.
Classification: LCC PT2664.O53 W3613 2023 | DDC 831/.914--dc23/eng/20221006
LC record available at https://lccn.loc.gov/2022046877

Cover and book design: Christopher Nelson

Green Linden Press is a nonprofit publisher dedicated to fostering
excellent poetry and supporting reforestation with a portion of proceeds.

CONTENTS

~⚬~

Poems

die Antwort muß ja sein können

the answer yes must be possible

Hilde Domin

~✦~

For all in these unsteady times
who find themselves searching for a haven from violence
and freedom from repression

Denn wir essen Brot, aber wir leben von Glanz.

For we eat bread, but we live from radiance.[1]

Hilde Domin

∼◦∽

FOREWORD

Why Poetry Still Today? The Poetry of Hilde Domin[1]
by Marion Tauschwitz

> This wide wing
> my word
> with the invisible pinions
> I've gone far I've run
> with lidless eyes
> up the continents the years
>
> —Hilde Domin, "This Wide Wing"[2]

In 1940 when Hilde Palm[3] sought refuge as a young Jewish emigrant in the Dominican Republic, orphaned and homeless "at the edge of the world where pepper plants grew and sugarcane and mango trees, but where roses barely survived,"[4] all that was left to her was the word. The German word. That saved her when she was expelled from yesterday, when today wasn't meant for her and tomorrow was uncertain. The German language became her bulwark against what had become an unlivable reality. That word remained dependable even when love abandoned her in this dark period. And the word carried her as the world around her collapsed; she wrote, "I stepped into the air, and it carried me."[5]

One finds forms of experience woven into Hilde Domin's poetry because as a poet she strode through life with "lidless eyes" that had not shut themselves to reality. She wanted to be "split open as from a lightning bolt" from that which she saw. For only in this way could her experiences find their way into images that burned themselves into the "retina" of remembering until they formed themselves into an amalgam of yearning for freedom and hope.[6] The scars from her experience of exile, though, were not healed, and each similarly painful situation in life opened the old wounds again.

Their return to Germany in 1954 was for Hilde Domin and her husband, Erwin Walter Palm, an experience of utmost fragility. To exchange the feeling of return for the feeling of being-at-home called for fresh courage: the courage of forgiveness. The courage to create their homeland anew, to open professional opportunities after having been denied success over the years. Only in 1959 did

Domin make her breakthrough as a writer with the publication of her first collection of poems, *Only a Rose for Support.*[7] When the philosopher Hans-Georg Gadamer subsequently called her "the poet of the return," this was balm for those German souls who saw her, as a Jewish-born poet, as one who after her return was prepared to forgive and thus purportedly mitigated their German guilt. Jewish colleagues, and above all the poet Paul Celan, held this against her. The initial euphoria over her first book of poems was followed by years of struggle against the male-dominated literary scene of the times, which threatened to sink her. This demanded perseverance of her.

Even though the language and the trust that her family had instilled within her became her irrevocable "portable homeland," the outward homelessness she faced made her a seeker, one who spent her entire life journeying and "on the move," in both a spiritual and physical sense. This is how I came to know her in 2001. She became my friend despite the vast difference in our age. Though elderly, she was still energetic. Unconventional. With a sharp mind and as young at heart as she was in her view of the world. Her life remained restless as if she remained in flight, as if her life were but a "rendezvous with the moment."[8] I experienced her as both fragile and unshakable—always a rose at a precipice, one that protected her secret until her death.

Oh, this rose—the "experience of a fleeting existence," Hilde Domin once said to me. This rose bloomed during many intimate conversations I had with her. Above all when the cheerfulness of the afternoons fled and mysteries crept out in the twilight of those blue hours. At such times, I sought to strip the petals of the rose in order to coax the mystery from it. This revealed itself to me only after her death.

Hilde Domin's poetry moved me deeply already during my early years as a university student. Suffering and comfort alike found voice in her poems, but it was their authenticity above all that drew me. They enchanted me with the "sacred breath" that seemed to pour forth from them, making it clear that the poet stayed at her writing—as she put it in a letter to her husband—until "the voices of the tormented were transformed into beautiful music."[9] Poems became a solace, becoming what she called "songs of encouragement," because she refused to remain in pain and countered melancholy and lament with a defiant "nevertheless" (*dennoch*) that had the capacity of wresting consolation even from misery.

Her earliest poems were witnesses, above all, to her inner "soulscape" (*Seelenlandschaft*), written as they had been during the agonizing time she spent in Haiti (1952–53). For during that period of her life, she found herself—beyond her outward exile—expelled from "the house of love" when her husband threatened to leave her. I came to sense this only when she later referred to me as her "younger sister" because, as she put it, "only my blood is coursing through you, and not Erwin's."[10]

I discovered the full extent to which Hilde Domin's early poems gave poetic expression to personal experiences of her own—voicing themes such as loneliness, persecution, terror, grief, yearning for love—only after her death when, in the course of my research for her biography, I read through the thousands of letters she had written during her lifetime.

The poet took what she experienced and forged it into poetry, and in so doing conveyed experiences in ways that made them generally applicable for others; by omitting the outward "facts," she "de-individualized" the most intimate images from her life. Like a gardener, she pruned, cut, and streamlined such personal strands, lending her poems a distinctly modern feeling.

Because she never revealed herself as a poet by detailing the facts of her life, her poems acquired the striking characteristic of an *unspecific exactness*, which gives them a timeless quality and allows readers to make her poems their own. They become "magical objects of use" for me.[11] They acquire thereby an applicability for others, inviting readers to an encounter with themselves.

This is how readers received her poetry after the publication of her first collection, *Only a Rose for Support*. As poems inspiring courage (*mutmachende Verse*), having the power to name our innermost realities without directly revealing them. Readers loved the tender breath of her simple language that wasted no effort on a muddled use of metaphor, and that made her language light and open and comforting. "The pale, damaged heart is raised up and laid out in the early sun."[12] Her "simple words smell of humans."[13] They light a fire; they get under the skin by making experiences immediately relatable.

And where is Hilde Domin's place in the history of German literature? On a freestanding branch between Bertolt Brecht and Gottfried Benn, she sprouts as a powerful leaf and flourishes alongside Marie Luise Kaschnitz, Karl Krolow, Günter Eich, and Peter Huchel. Greening forth and sending out blossoms. A rare plant among writers. With much "world" but little ground underfoot. An author living and writing among several languages, cultures, and literary influences, who wrote in both German and Spanish, was influenced by the Arabic legacy of Spain and the Italian writer Giuseppe Ungaretti, who was himself influenced by Egyptian sources. Late in her life, Domin opened herself to the inspiration of Japanese aesthetics—a mix that carries the power of survival from which a way of living and not simply a way of working speaks. A tightrope artist, she "stepped into the air, and it carried" her.

INTRODUCTION

"I Went Home in the Word"
by Mark S. Burrows

Poetry is like a great pealing of bells: so that everyone takes notice.
So that each one who does so listens for that which serves no pur-
pose and would be falsified through compromise. And this holds
for the most despairing poem, and even for a poem that is negative
and maddening: it is a pealing of bells. In truth, there is no poem
"against" that is not at the same time and to a greater extent "for":
as an appeal for helpers in order to overcome, together, something
unlivable. And therein lies the catharsis: in an ultimate faith in hu-
manity, without which there could be no poetry.

—Hilde Domin[1]

In the middle of her life, Hilde Domin published an autobiographical essay that
began with a startling claim: "I, H.D., am surprisingly young. I first came into
the world in 1951."[2] This confession was not meant to confuse but to clarify,
pointing to the new identity she discovered at that time, which she came to
refer to as her "second life."[3] She went on to speak of the Dominican Republic
as her birthplace, the land where she and her husband had been welcomed as
Jewish refugees in 1940:

Like everyone else, I came weeping into this world. It was not in
Germany, though German is my mother-tongue. There, Spanish was
spoken and the garden in front of our house was lined with coco-
nut palms. More precisely: eleven palm trees, all of them masculine,
meaning they bore no fruit. My parents were dead when I entered
the world. My mother had died only a few weeks before my birth.

She then turns from this strange account to admit that

naturally, of course, I had always been there. "Always," in this case,
reaches back to the years just before the so-called First [World] War.
Naturally, my parents were then alive; naturally, German was spoken
and the nanny, whom I don't remember, was certainly not a person

of color, just as the row of trees in front of the house were ordinary trees—maples, I believe. In front of the house stood, and still stands, a small, Japanese almond tree.[4]

The title she gave to that essay, "Among Acrobats and Birds," captures the sense of dislocation she faced during the years of her exile.[5] In the poem from which she borrowed this title, she sketched the precariousness of her situation:

> I furnish[ed] a room in the air
> among acrobats and birds:
> my bed on the trapeze of feeling
> like a nest in the wind
> on the branches' outermost tips.[6]

With such stark images, Domin captured the vulnerability of exile as well as the unsettling mix of terror and exhilaration it carried. She went on to recall how she discovered her identity in the German language in the months immediately following her mother's death in 1951, marked by an outpouring of poems that came unannounced. The magnitude of this experience led her to describe it as "a second birth."[7] Only several years later, after gaining confidence in her vocation as a writer, did she find the courage to return to Germany after an exile that had lasted more than two decades:

> When I opened [my] eyes, filled with tears, in that house at the edge of the world where pepper plants grew and sugarcane and mango trees, but where roses barely survived and where apples, wheat, and birch trees were not to be found, I who had been orphaned and banished stood up and went home in the word. "I furnished a room in the air / among acrobats and birds," and from there could not be banished. But the word was German, and for that reason I later traveled back across the sea to the place where that word lived. This was three years after my birth; I had been gone for twenty-two years.[8]

Her sense of "[going] home in the word" points to how language itself—or, more precisely, the language of her birth—offered her what she longed for: a measure of security, or "*Geborgenheit*," an untranslatable German noun whose verbal root suggests "being sheltered," "held tenderly," even "saved."[9] Over the years of her exile, that yearning pointed to what she lacked: the stability of *Heimat*, a word suggesting not a "place" but rather a sense of "being-at-home," a free rendering of this translation-defying word. The cascade of poems that came to her at that time were like floodwaters bursting through a weakened dam. But if writing became the means of Domin's "rebirth," the experience of exile remained within her as an ineradicable part of her identity. This "unlosable exile," she later wrote, is something "you carry...within you, wilderness, portable."[10]

The experience of exile as a "portable wilderness" and the longing for homeland became the warp and weft of Domin's identity, early and late. Each represented in its own manner an unsettling sense of vulnerability and loss; she had, after all, been "orphaned and driven out," as she described the plight that left her without a "fatherland," a predicament she described with the neologism "*vaterlandslos*."[11] As interwoven themes, exile and homeland gave shape and momentum to her vocation as a writer, offering her a way to make "an appeal for helpers in order to overcome, together, something unlivable."[12]

What gradually became clear to her was that this "second chance" was not simply for her but also for the wounded culture—and language—from which she had been exiled.[13] On the strength of that chance, she was one of the few Jewish writers and intellectuals of her generation who, having either escaped or survived the Holocaust, chose to return to live in Germany after the war. That decision took an act of courage, given the horrors of the preceding decades, but she refused to see it simply as a gesture of defiance. She came to understand it as expressing "an ultimate faith in humanity, without which there could be no poetry." As she later put it, "my poems are a call to take responsibility."[14]

Domin insisted that each of her books—and, finally, every poem of hers— was to be read as a "*Befreiungsakt*," or "liberating act," calling her and her readers to look ahead with hope and not behind with bitterness or regret.[15] The surname she took upon returning to Germany in 1954 bore witness to that conviction: "Domin" became the *nom de plume* by which she publicly declared her new-found identity, signifying her gratitude to the country where she and her husband had found if not *Heimat* then at least a threshold of *Geborgenheit*. She gave voice to that unexpected and unlikely discovery when she later wrote, "I stepped into the air, and it carried me."[16] These terse lines point to a certainty she sensed amid uncertain circumstances, since a "foothold" of this sort, if one could call it that, was tenuous at best. But "it carried" her.

In point of fact, her birthname was Hildegard Dina Löwenstein. Hilde, as she came to be called, was born on July 27, 1909, and died nearly a century later on February 22, 2006. Her parents were part of the large and self-assured Jewish community in the city of Cologne and made their home in a spacious and well-appointed apartment in Riehlerstraße 23, a place she described as "a very bourgeois house."[17] She grew up there with her younger brother Hans, enjoying a life grounded in "a familial security" (*eine familiäre Geborgenheit*): "There, my parents provided [us] with trust, a primal trust (*Urvertrauen*) that seemed indestructible and from which I take the power of the 'nevertheless' (*dennoch*)."[18] It was this internal inheritance that shaped her life and determined the tenor of her writing. Honoring this legacy long after both of her parents had died, she voiced her admiration and respect for them by dedicating her *Gesammelte Aufsätze. Heimat in der Sprache (Collected Essays. Homeland in Language)* to their memory: "For my parents, who equipped me to endure life in this [20th] century."[19]

Tutored privately until the age of eleven, Hilde attended her first school when her parents enrolled her in the Merlo-Mevissen-Lyzeum. Upon graduation she matriculated at the University of Heidelberg in 1929 to study law. It soon became apparent, however, that this choice—"inspired by my father," she remarked, who had served as an attorney and public defender in Cologne— would be short-lived. After her first semester she switched faculties, turning her attention to political science and sociology. She eventually returned to Cologne following a serious illness, and after an interrupted semester of study there and in nearby Bonn, she moved to Berlin to continue her studies at the Humboldt University in the winter semester of 1930.

Berlin during the years of the Weimar Republic (1918–33) had become a hotbed of radical politics and contentious political debates, and Hilde Löwenstein found herself thrust into the thick of this turbulence. Shortly after she arrived, she heard Thomas Mann—recently honored with the Nobel Prize in Literature, in 1929—deliver a daring public lecture entitled "An Appeal to Reason," warning, amid loud heckling from some in the audience, of the menace posed by the National Socialist Party and Hitler's growing popularity. In early December, 1930, she went with other students to hear Hitler give a public speech, having just read *Mein Kampf* that fall, encounters that convinced her that "what Hitler described there he would surely carry out."[20] That semester in Berlin had a deep effect on her, alerting her to the ominous storms gathering force in Germany.

In the spring of 1931, she moved back to Heidelberg where she met Erwin Walter Palm, a student of ancient philology and archaeology. They fell in love and decided to move to Italy together later that year with the authorization of a *"Heimatschein für den Aufenthalt im Ausland"* in hand, a two-year visa from the German government allowing them to study abroad. Already during the early months of their stay, however, it became clear that they could not return to Germany: the increasing violence of the Nazi campaign to eradicate citizens of Jewish descent destroyed that hope altogether. After a brief initial stay in Rome, the couple moved to Florence, completing advanced degrees in 1935 before deciding the following year to marry. Their wedding in Rome on October 30, 1936, was the last time the Löwensteins would gather for a family celebration. Noticeably absent was Hilde's brother Hans who had decided to emigrate to the United States and had already left for New York earlier that month; her parents arrived from Paris having fled from Cologne in October, 1933, first seeking refuge in Belgium before moving to France.

During the years of their forced exile in Italy, they "survived, literally, on language," as Hilde Palm later put it. Alongside completing her studies and assisting her husband with his work, she taught German language courses from mornings until evenings to help make ends meet. Their second exile followed several years later as the situation for Jews continued to deteriorate under Mussolini's fascist regime. As foreigners with Jewish heritage, they had no chance of gaining Italian citizenship, but initially felt safe enough to remain in Italy even as events in Germany worsened, particularly after the "Race Laws" of 1935. The Italian Parliament followed suit, however, enacting its own "Race Laws" in 1938, leaving them no choice but to flee. They fled from Italy at the last possible moment, in March, 1939, making their way first to Paris and then on to England where they joined Hilde's parents, who by then had resettled in the small town of Minehead on the Somerset coast.

After the capitulation of France to the Nazis on June 22, 1940, Hilde and Erwin Palm decided to leave England for greater safety elsewhere. They set forth from Liverpool several days later, on June 26, 1940, aboard the steamship "Scythia" bound for Canada:

> I travel
> toward islands without harbors,
> I throw the keys into the sea
> as soon as I depart.
> I arrive nowhere.
> My sail is like a cobweb in the wind,
> but it doesn't tear.
> And beyond the horizon
> where the great birds
> dry their wings in the sun
> at the end of their migration
> there's a continent
> where they must take me in
> without a passport,
> on the clouds' guarantee.[21]

They eventually found a harbor of safe haven in the Dominican Republic where they were to remain for more than a decade. During those years, with a tenuous security depending on the vagaries of "the clouds' guarantee," as she later put it, Hilde Palm devoted herself to supporting her husband's career, serving as his secretary, assisting him with the photographs needed for his research, and joining him in several translation projects—all this alongside her work as a German language instructor at the University of Santo Domingo (1948–52).

Their personal lives during these years of exile were not without troubles, and during a period of growing marital estrangement, shortly after the death of her mother in 1951, she began to write—in large part, as she later put it, to ward off suicidal urges. Writing offered her the sense of the *Geborgenheit* she increasingly failed to find in her marriage, which had begun to feel like its own form of exile with little hope of refuge.[22] In the years after her mother's passing and the "new beginning" that followed, she wrote what she later described as "hundreds of poems."[23] Over the next several years, in fact, her writing became the central occupation of her life, giving her the sense of security she longed for and finally found—as a "homeland in language" (*Heimat in der Sprache*), as she later put it, while still living in exile.

The early 1950s offered her what she came to understand as a "second chance." It was then that Hilde Palm took the surname "Domin" to express her debt to the country that had offered them refuge after their flight from Europe in 1940. In an early poem entitled "Allowed to Land," she described coming to that decision:

> I named myself
> I personally called myself
> by the name of an island.
>
> It is the name of a Sunday
> of a dreamt-of island.
> Columbus discovered the island
> on a Christmas Sunday.
>
> It was a coastline
> a place to land
> one could step onto it
> the nightingales sing there on Christmas.
>
> Name yourself, someone said to me
> as I went ashore in Europe,
> with the name of your island.[24]

She later observed—as one who "went home in the word"—that she found her vocation as a writer as "one who was dying, who writes against dying." Her poetry became a saving presence in her life, giving her strength to shoulder the losses and betrayals she faced with the anguish and self-doubt they triggered. She voiced her experience of survival in a poem entitled "Pulling Landscape":

One must hold one's breath
until the wind abates
and the strange air around us begins to stir,
until the game of light and shadows,
green and blue,
shows its old pattern
and we find ourselves at home
wherever that might be,
and can sit down and lean back
as if on the grave
of our mother.[25]

In the summer of 1952, Domin left Santo Domingo for Haiti, alone, following a crisis in her marriage. She there found refuge in a mountain hotel located a short distance from Port-au-Prince, describing the intense self-discovery of this period in a lengthy poem entitled "*Wen es trifft*" ("Whom It Concerns"):

The terrible pause
in the ordeal
sinks in
like the depths between islands.
The barriers
at all the borders
are transposed into the light
as in dreams after an operation.
But the substance
of the I
is as different
as metal as it comes forth from a blast furnace.
Or as if that I
fell from the tenth or twentieth floor
—the difference matters little
in the case of such a death-defying leap—
landing on its feet
in the middle of Times Square
just managing
to avoid the cars' bumpers
before the lights turned red.
But a certain lightness
remained
with the I
like a bird.[26]

After the two had reunited the following year, they moved together to New York City where Erwin had received a Guggenheim Fellowship that provided funds for a six-month residency. During the months that followed their arrival in the United States, however, their marital difficulties intensified yet again, and in the early summer of 1953, Hilde left New York—and Erwin—for northern New England. She rented a small cottage on the island of Vinalhaven, off the coast of Rockland, Maine, later recalling the months she spent alone there as among the happiest of her life.[27] Erwin followed her in September, hoping to salvage their marriage.

The following February, back in New York, the Palms reunited, again, and made the momentous decision to return not to the Caribbean but to now-divided Germany. Much had changed there since they had left as students in 1932, and their long exile from Europe had changed them as well. Domin later described the ambivalence of their experience arriving back after what had become a twenty-two-year exile:

> You eat memories
> with the spoon of forgetting.
>
> It is a wicked spoon with which you eat,
> a spoon that consumes food and eater,
>
> Until a peel of shadows
> remains for you
> in a shadow-hand.[28]

After arriving back in Germany, they eventually returned to Cologne and found their way to Domin's childhood home. The building was still largely intact, though the entire row of houses on the street's opposite side had been destroyed during the war and, like much of the city, still lay in ruins. It was mid-February, but the Japanese almond tree in front of the house which she remembered from her youth was already in bloom. She interpreted it as an auspicious sign:

> By the house of my childhood
> the almond tree bloomed
> in February.
>
> I had dreamt
> that it would bloom.[29]

When they approached the front door, however, they found an unfamiliar name on the nameplate where "Löwenstein" had once been inscribed. After ringing the same worn-out doorbell she remembered from her childhood, they entered the entrance hall and passed the familiar letterbox before ascending the worn marble stairs that led to what had been the family's second-floor apartment. The exterior of the building was largely intact, but much had changed inside: the spacious apartment where she had grown up had been subdivided after the war to make room for two smaller units. Yet much remained the same, and she immediately fell to her knees, as she had often done as a child, in front of the "*Jugendstil*" fireplace in the living room to the bewilderment of the seamstress then living in the Löwensteins' former home.

Reflecting on that visit in a later essay she admitted that "to return—that is something entirely different than what one expects. Our memory stretches a web of entirely uneven stitches through our heart….When one has spent an entire life elsewhere and then returns home, it is not as if a bucket of water were poured out into a pond. What is essential is surely the experience of different realities—almost as if a statue had fallen into the hands of one sculptor after another, each of whom worked it over anew. One loses—and gains."[30] Neither the Löwensteins' Cologne nor Frankfurt of the Palm family was to become their home, however, and in any event the couple's return to Germany was short-lived: they left for Spain the following year so that Erwin could continue his work on the Iberian art and architecture of the colonial period. Only then, years after having begun this work in Santo Domingo, was he able to publish the academic books he had completed—with Hilde's assistance—during the preceding decade.

The years that followed in Madrid were to be significant for Domin's fledgling career as a writer as she began to publish her own poems and translations in various journals—both in Spain and in Germany, and in both Spanish and German. In 1957, however, she left Spain and her husband to return a second time to Germany. Her acquaintance with Rudolf Hirsch, whom she had met among other German publishers and writers during her years in Madrid, proved decisive for her professional identity as a poet: as the publisher of S. Fischer Verlag in Frankfurt, he was instrumental in helping to launch her public career as a writer.[31] As she later put it, "from the beginnings of a correspondence concerning lines of poetry, a relationship [to this press] grew of its own volition."[32] Finally, after having had success publishing in various literary journals, both in Spain and in Germany, Hirsch offered to publish her first book of poems, a volume that appeared in 1959—after Domin had returned to Spain—under the title *Only a Rose for Support*.

This proved decisive for her professional recognition and public reception as a writer. In one of the earliest reviews of this volume, published shortly after the book's publication,[33] the prominent literary critic and professor of rhetoric at the University of Tübingen, Walter Jens, praised the collection as written by "one of the most important, though until today little-known [German] authors" of the day. Introducing her as "a poet who understood to wait," he characterized her poems as "filled with music and grace, but also bound by a strong sense of intelligence and great clarity."[34] Jens' early endorsement would be amply confirmed over the decades that followed. Indeed, over the course of her long career as a writer, Domin came to be counted among the prominent literary voices of post-war Germany.

A little more than a decade later, in 1971, the distinguished philosopher Hans-Georg Gadamer published an essay appreciative of her poetry entitled "*Hilde Domin, Dichterin der Rückkehr*" ("Hilde Domin, Poet of the Return").[35] At the beginning of the next decade, Karl Krolow contributed a further study of Domin's poetry under the title "*Ich will einen Streifen Papier*" ("I Want a Scrap of Paper"), taking the title from a line in her poem "Three Ways to Write Poems Down," where he praised her writing by pointing to "a passionate self-development comprised of drifting delights" found in it.[36]

She went on to receive a string of prestigious literary honors and prizes during the last decades of her life.[37] Poet and novelist Ulla Hahn wrote the *Laudatio* for Domin's reception of the Friedrich Hölderlin Prize in 1992, celebrating her as a "poet of the 'nevertheless' (*dennoch*)" who seized the chance to start a "second life," going on to extoll her poetry as shimmering with "an unspecific exactness" and to praise her determination, in spite of obstacles and difficulties, "to love nevertheless" (*dennoch lieben*).[38] Several years later, in 1995, she received the Literature Prize of the Konrad Adenauer Foundation, delivered in the Goethe House in Weimar, and on that occasion Marcel Reich-Ranicki praised her poems for the way they remained "utterly devoid of decoration and hysteria" and were "at once cool and quiet and sovereign in a marvelous manner."[39]

By the time of her death, her poems and essays, though translated into twenty-three languages, had been generally neglected by English translators and thus remained largely unknown to non-German readers.[40] In one of the exceptions to this lacuna, and only in the year of her death in 2006, British literary critic Ben Hutchinson hailed her poetry for the ways it "seeks to eschew sentimentality and remain light and beguilingly naïve, 'hand in hand with language / to the last': 'The tree still blossoms / Trees have always blossomed / even for executions.'" Citing these lines from the title poem of her final collection, *Der Baum blüht trotzdem* (*The Tree Blooms Regardless*), Hutchinson went on to highlight, as typical of her poetry, "the juxtaposition of rootedness with a moment of fugitive beauty, of horror with a moment of defiance."[41]

In 1960, Erwin Palm finally secured a university appointment in Heidelberg, for Portuguese and Spanish colonial art. The following February, upon completing work on her first novel after having rejoined her husband in Madrid, Domin returned to live in the city where she had begun her studies more than three decades earlier.[42] After more than two decades of exile and much of a third spent in an itinerancy between Germany and Spain, she had finally found what became her home for the last forty-five years of her life. During that nearly half-century, she established herself as a prominent voice in the German literary scene, publishing—among other books—seven collections of poetry, including the posthumously published *Sämtliche Gedichte* (*Complete Poems*), a novel, a collection of short stories, and two studies of poetics.[43] Over the span of those five decades, she also received numerous distinguished awards and prizes for her work, including—alongside those already mentioned—the Rainer Maria Rilke Prize for Poetry in 1976, the Nelly Sachs Prize given by the city of Dortmund in 1983, the Order of Merit of the Federal Republic of Germany in 1994, and a similar medal by the Dominican Republic in 2005, conveyed in the year before her death.[44]

Beginning with her first book of 1959, Domin quickly distinguished herself within German society both as a poet and as an interpreter of poetics, exploring in talks and essays the nature and function of poetry within society. The first volume she devoted to this topic appeared in 1968. In response to the turmoil of that decade, Domin staked out a defiant, counter-cultural apology for poetry, arguing against strident voices that had largely dismissed it as an expendable luxury. Leaning on Hölderlin's brooding question, "Why poets in destitute times?," she entitled her manifesto *Why Poetry Today. Poetry and readers in a managed society.*[45] Focusing on the function of poetry rather than the role of the poet, her critique answered those who dismissed literature as serving no purpose in the face of the social unrest and political crises of the day. In the process, Domin articulated a bold rebuttal to Theodor Adorno's contentious and much-discussed indictment of 1949, that "to write a poem after Auschwitz was barbaric." Domin saw things differently:

> We find ourselves in a dilemma. What would literature be—and above all, poetry—if it did not locate itself within this dilemma? Literature can be nothing other than we ourselves and the circumstances in which we must live. The desire to articulate inhumanity is a mistaken desire; it must fail. Inhumanity can only be portrayed in terms of humanity. By what other means should it be measured? A new equilibrium between feeling and understanding, a new sensibil-

ity for language—not only for language, but surely and above all on its behalf—is long overdue. Away from the daily feeding of hollow words of any kind.[46]

Some twenty years later she published a second treatise on poetics in her capacity as guest professor at the University of Frankfurt, an appointment she had received for the winter semester of 1987–88. The central obligation of that professorship was to deliver the Frankfurt Lectures on Poetics, a lectureship that had been suspended during the decade following 1968. Each of her five lectures attracted a capacity audience that filled the university's largest auditorium long before the time appointed for the talks to begin.[47]

Domin opened the first of these—published in 1988 as *Das Gedicht als Augenblick von Freiheit* (*The Poem as a Moment of Freedom*)—wondering whether she should not rather speak of poems as "a moment of liberation" (*ein Moment der Befreiung*). Over the course of these lectures she returned to a theme she had earlier announced in *Why Poetry Today*, arguing against those who, in her mind, had prematurely announced the "death of poetry." She reminded her hearers that her earlier book had only recently been reissued with a new cover, highlighting her conviction in bold print that poetry offered "Breathing Room for Freedom" (*Atemraum für Freiheit*).[48] She went on in that lecture to suggest that the cultural needs of the times—the late 1980s—required what she called "an 'active pause' in which we find ourselves as a subject rather than an object."[49] Freedom for her meant responsibility, of course, but only through such a perspectival "pause" could poetry become the needed counterforce against what she disparagingly called "an automatizing culture driven by men standing in front of, behind, and next to [that society]."[50]

If the essays collected in *Why Poetry Today* embroiled her in the heated anti-literary culture debates of the 1960s, her Frankfurt Lectures delivered two decades later met an attentive and sympathetic audience. The times had changed. Many of those in attendance were students of a generation removed from the tumult of the late 1960s. Their concerns were hardly apolitical, given the accelerating tensions of the Cold War with the acute threat of nuclear conflict, but perhaps for that very reason they seemed receptive to Domin's determination to "call what devours by name," citing an apocalyptic reference from an ancient Hebrew Psalm:

> calling each other
> with the small voice
> to call what devours by name
> with nothing but our breath
>
> save us from the mouth of the lion[51]

In such unsettled times, Domin turned headlong into the storm, provocatively entitling her opening lecture "The stopping of time and purpose.—Phases of German post-war poetry as depicted by those in this country, and to those who have returned home [from exile]." In clarifying her identity as one of the latter, she declared "how central the question of poetry" had been in her life, reminding her hearers—and later readers—that she was one "who had experienced exile and persecution [and] should not be seen as 'living in an ivory tower', but as one aware of life's contradictions, and, far from shying away from them, one who strives to face them directly."[52] Her poetry, she reminded her audience, came out of the experience of persecution and still carried shadows from the "portable wilderness" of exile. Yet it did so by answering that world in the face of such suffering with the "nevertheless" that had become for her—and for her readers—a resilient source of hope.

In her writings as in her public addresses over the long decades of her career, Domin established herself as "the poet of the 'nevertheless' (dennoch)," a writer whose poems gave expression to "the flashing contradictoriness of [their] oppositions."[53] Indeed, through her long experience of exile and the longing for "homeland" this brought with it, she had come to understand "the poem, like humans themselves, as a 'shifting merger of the un-unite-able', a field of tensions made up of its possibilities. Either/or: this alternative does not exist [for poems]. The poem is always situated between the two."[54] She went on to depict the poet's vocation as living in answer to "the call against programmability": "Ultimately," she insisted, "the poems I seek to deliver are all 'nevertheless'-poems (Dennoch-Gedichte)."[55]

In referring to the title of the section "Songs of Encouragement" from her second published collection, Rückkehr der Schiffe (Return of the Ships, 1962), Domin interpreted these "songs" as "the inverse of the theme of loss: the gift that [our] hands fail to hold. I don't know with what [we] should take it up. Only that it is an extreme, a borderline luck [ein Grenzglück], the most fragile" of things.[56] She went on to recall the opening lines from the lead poem in her first collection, "Pulling Landscape," which began with an image fraught with stark contradictions:

> One must be able to depart
> and yet remain like a tree:
> as if the roots remained in the ground,
> as if the landscape pulled and we stood still.[57]

In commenting on these tensions, she suggested that

> the opposite of the expected transpires here, as there, in the border images we find in life's borderline situations. One might well ask, "How is one to do this?" This cannot, but nevertheless [*dennoch*] must, be done if one is not to lose oneself entirely. The paradoxes of exile, the identity crisis par excellence. *Exilium vita est,* one finds inscribed above the front door of Victor Hugo's house on Guernsey. An ancient wisdom. Life is an exile. Exile is thus the characteristic situation of our humanity.[58]

She captures this tension in a suggestive—one might even say "programmatic"—short poem from this collection:

> Our pillows are wet
> with the tears
> of dreams destroyed.
>
> But once again
> the dove
> rises from our empty
> helpless hands.[59]

In later commenting on this poem, she insisted that "this 'dove' does not come from nothing, but from a peculiar something. It cannot come from empty hands. But that it does precisely this is the main thing: the tipping point [*Kippsituation*] on the boundary of reality that I've spoken of—that is, paradox."[60] She recognized that this conviction set her apart from many of her contemporaries and from most of those who had been exiled during the 1930s and '40s. Speaking of herself as an "exceptional situation," she admitted that

> if everyone sees things as Kafka did, who said that his dove had returned home and had found "nothing green," my poems see with wide-open eyes how plundered the fields are and how bare the branches. How everything is empty. And yet out of fear they fly so far and so high that they somewhere discover a blue or green—already entirely transparent. As we do, in actuality, again and again, because otherwise we would no longer be living. The purely negative (*das Nur-Negative*) is a posture.[61]

Against such a posture, Domin identified herself as a poet whose vocation it was to bear witness to "new beginnings," a claim she lived out over the last half-century of her life as a writer. Indeed, the title of the fifth and final of her

Frankfurt Lectures might well stand as an epigraph of her life: "Sisyphus: the daily exertion to do the impossible.— The writing refugee as an exceptional instance of the Sisyphus-existence.— The postulate of the *second chance*: The new beginning." She opened that lecture with this short poem:

> Who could do it
> throw the world
> so high
> that the wind
> could pass through it.[62]

In an essay first published in 1961, which looked back at her life as a refugee in the face of having returned to her *Heimat* in Germany, Domin described her experience in "becoming Hilde Domin" this way:

> In the time when I became Hilde Domin, with all these years of wandering from country to country, from one language-region to another, all of which suddenly presented themselves as preparation, as instructional years, I worked as a lecturer in German at the University of Santo Domingo. My first poem closed with the lines:
>
> > And a great blooming arose
> > shining faintly
> > from my heart
>
> Since then, my writing is for me like breathing: one dies if one relinquishes it.[63]

Later in the same essay she went on to describe her vocation as a "poet of the second chance" by pointing to the actual "use" readers made of her poems:

> When I began writing [poetry] in 1951, it seemed to me—as it does to every writer—that everything previously [written] belonged to a pre-history....It is a fact that my poems belong to those that are read. In other words, they have been "used." I don't believe, though, that poems are an "object of use" [*Gebrauchsgegenstand*] like those that can be "used up." Rather, they belong to those magical "objects of use" which, like the body of a lover, come to flourish in being drawn upon.[64]

She went on to argue against any tendency that saw *art pour l'art*, insisting that

> Poetry is there for everyone, and renews itself with each reader. Experiences that readers read into poems are often conveyed to oth-

ers, even to the next generation of readers....For this reason a living poem changes itself and becomes new and different, even for its author who can later read it differently than on the day when it was first written.[65]

Yet one finds throughout the long arc of her poems a voice Walter Jens had described, at the outset of her career, as one of "perfection in plainness" (*Vollkommenheit im Einfachen*).[66] But that simplicity was one of "*Raffinement*," as he went on to say. What distinguishes her poetic voice is her startling use of metaphor, unexpected twists of diction, and a syntax often compressed to the point of abruptness. She eschewed rhyme and meter in favor of free verse from the start, and by her third collection (*Hier*), published in 1964, had abandoned punctuation almost entirely. The temperament of her poems depends on a distinct musicality shaped largely by the rhythm of speech. Plainness? Perhaps, but one carried by a sense of "fullness" that demands readers' attention in "listening" their way into the sound and pace of her voice—and their own.

Over the long arc of her career as a writer, Domin's poems gave shape to her belief that our vocation as humans is to cultivate "the second chance"—for ourselves, yes, but also and always on behalf of others. She articulated this conviction eloquently in a 1982 address entitled "Advice for Graduates" for students of the Freiherr-von-Stein-Schule in Leverkusen. She exhorted them to

> give the other a chance, for he has as much fear for you as you do for him....Not "refusal." Relinquishment is the law of this historical moment. Relinquishment of one's own advantage. Relinquishment of needing to be "in," always and everywhere. For relinquishment is freeing. Relinquishment of every use of clichéd language that hides reality. Detachment, looking closely, looking with exactness. Naming oneself. Being ready for the moment in which time stands still. In which a person becomes themselves. Fully themselves, for only then are they able to become one with the other. This is the paradox: time only exists when it ceases: in the pause. Only an "I" can be brother to their neighbor.[67]

Dialogical to the core, she went on to appeal to "a sober, unguarded kind of emancipation: without retreating. Abandoning no one who trusts you. I advocate for that which is uncomfortable, which is practiced on the far side of slogans: without publicity and without noise. The miracle, the concrete, small miracle waits around the next corner for those who are ready to perceive it."[68]

What was—and is—this "miracle"? It might be something as small and private as a gesture of generosity, or as public as her defense of exiles in later times—the so-called "boat-people" fleeing Viet Nam during the mid-1970s[69]—and her opposition to the stranglehold of what she called the "managed society" (*die gesteuerte Gesellschaft*) of late-modern capitalism. In the face of such oppressive forces, as she put it in an early poem dedicated to her first publisher, Rudolf Hirsch, the miracles were still present:

> And yet after going a long way,
> the miracle won't fail to appear,
> because the miracle is always happening,
> and because we cannot live
> without grace...[70]

Her claim is significant. But if these "miracles" are "always happening," she also knew that they were discoverable only by those who had attuned themselves to look for them—hence, her call for "the active 'pause.'" As she put it in a late poem, they reveal themselves by the radiance (*Glanz*) they carry. In the closing stanzas of "Between Always and Always," she points to the traces of what she calls

> the wandering radiance
> the large slow hand that
> unrelentingly caressing
> strokes you above the eternal heart
> doesn't pause
> and pushes the hours away
> on the clockface of your shoreline
>
> With her index finger made of shadow and gold
> she signals the birds to keep silent
> in the wide palm-basket of the night
> and redeems the gift of this day
> from the tender short
> blossom-holiday
> of the gentle mimosas[71]

These are the same "miracles" described in a poem that ranks among her most beloved, "Don't Grow Weary":

> Don't grow weary
> but hold your hand out
> quietly

> to the miracle
> as if to a bird[72]

Domin understood poems as helping us, against our inclination toward indifference, to open our eyes to human need around us. This is the miracle, expressing as it does the momentum of her *nevertheless*-poetics.

Domin's poetry invites us to give ourselves over to that flight, to risk reaching for the "*Geborgenheit*" that is always in our midst—whether in exile or through our longing to "be-at-home" (*Heimat*). For the miracle, which "is always happening, / and because we cannot live / without grace," is as near to us as the human yearning for freedom, our own and that of others. Poems exist to awaken us to the urgencies of the moment, as she put it in her poem "Abel Get Up," a poem that voices a poetic midrash on the ancient biblical story of Cain and Abel:

> Abel get up
> it must be done again
> every day it must be done again
> every day the answer must be before us
> the answer yes must be possible
> if you don't get up Abel
> how should the answer
> this answer which is the only important one
> ever change
> …Get up every day
> so that we have this before us
> this Yes I am here
> I
> your brother

In an essay published eighteen years after she had written this poem, Domin insisted that "everything for me depends on this always-possible new beginning: the second chance. Which is provided for every person. That is the point of the poem 'Abel Get Up': a poem that is my ultimate word, and not only today."[73]

For Domin, having faced the difficult and painful experience of exile, Abel—the vulnerable one murdered by his brother Cain—became a sign of hope as one whose death could not, indeed must not, be seen as final. Through the anguish of loss and the bitterness of betrayal she came to see that only when we live responsibly, when we are here for each other—"This Yes, I am here / I / your brother"—can we discover together what it means to be human. Thus, while Domin held to the truth that "exile is the characteristic plight of our humanity," she insisted that we are also here for each other, stewards of the shared refuge—or *Heimat*—we all desire. And we come to do this through the ways we live in and share language, among other things, often enough against barbarities of various kinds.

This is the "return" she described in a late poem of the same name, which one might read as the credo of her vocation as a poet:

> I call the words back to me
> I lure all my words
> the helpless ones
>
> I gather the pictures
> the landscapes come to me
> the trees the people
>
> Nothing is far
> they all gather
> so much brightness
>
> I a part of them all
> return with all of them
> to myself
> and close myself
> and go forth
> out of the blossoming brightness
> out of the green the gold the blue
> into memorylessness[74]

Those who find themselves drawn by the lure of Domin's poems will understand her claim that "writing—and therefore reading—is a training in reality."[75] Whatever else poems "do," in whatever form they live within us, they remind us that "nothing is far." That we, too, no matter how deep the discouragements we face, have the capacity to "come home in the word." And that, when we do so, we discover dimensions by which we belong to each other, and to every other thing.

We need poems like these, in times like ours, as a needed counterweight to the widespread and growing experience of exile and bitter stories of persecution. We need them to remind us, when we find ourselves courted by despair or numbed by an indifference to the suffering of others, that we belong to each other. I can almost hear Hilde Domin reminding us that these poems need *us* as well: for they must be enacted, just as experiences of injustice often rooted in fundamental inequities remain for *us* to address. These poems call to us, encouraging us in the struggle to embody what it means to live together equitably in a world burdened with injustice, and to live peaceably in societies fraught with violence. They need *us* to resist cruelty within the wounded ecosystem to which we belong—together. And "therein lies the catharsis: in an ultimate faith in humanity, without which there could be no poetry."

Domin's poems remind us that we need words and actions able to gesture beyond our fears, that move us toward "the answer yes [that] must be possible." They point us, again and again, toward the "wandering radiance" that is always close to us—like "the large slow hand that / …pushes away the hours / on the clockface of [our] shoreline." We need poems like these that reassure us, in the midst of the shadows falling upon us, that the realities of our lives—our words, pictures, landscape, flowers, people—"all gather / so much brightness."

Mark S. Burrows

6 January 2023
Camden, Maine

Exile and Homeland[1]
by Hilde Domin

The central word in my life, in autobiographical terms as in the others, is trust: replenishing trust, resisting trust, nevertheless-trust [*Dennoch-Vertrauen*]… "Not to abandon—oneself or others—is the minimum-utopia without which it's not worth being human." I will hold fast to this commitment to my last breath.

Recently, when asked to give my view of things, I summarized my political "credo" after having lived such an exciting life—or, better: in the midst of this exciting life—like this:

> I believe that it is important to pass on not simply the memory of what we suffered, but also the memory of the help we received. And that we encourage young people never to look away from injustice, but always to face it, and always to try to change the world so that it might be more humane—not through ideologies, but rather so that each individual, where assistance is needed, turns to improve the fate of another.

For me there are no residual liabilities or privileges. Each generation must contribute what it can to the work of building a great community of remembering and helping, free of any contempt toward others. Only then can the suffering of this century become fruitful, on behalf of all the dead, for the sake of humanity.

<hr />

"Unlosable exile, you carry this within you, wilderness, portable," I once wrote upon arriving home again in Heidelberg. Homeland as the opposite of exile? No, that isn't right: exile is its opposite, its negation. Homeland would be what is self-evident, if it were self-evident. It is no accident, then, that in speaking of homeland I must start with exile. As if it were a kind of substitute-homeland [*Ersatzheimat*]. This is particularly true for me. And I will not do this because exile has become a "permissible" word, indeed a stylish word, while homeland must be articulated cautiously, as it has become practically a taboo to speak of it in these times. But someone in my circumstances does not bind themselves to such prohibitions. Above all not with respect to the matter of homeland, and indeed to the word itself. "Something that only appears in childhood, in which no one had yet been: homeland," as Ernst Bloch once put it. But he could just as well have said this of "paradise." His point was that it could not be banished, the security we have from the start [*die Geborgenheit von Anbeginn*]. The experience of being-allowed-to-belong [*Dazugehörendürfen*] *on this side* of doubt.

"One can love one's fatherland over the span of eighty years without having known it. But this is only so for those who never left home," Heinrich Heine once wrote. "The substance of spring is only recognizable in winter. Thus, the German love of the fatherland begins at the German border."

Already at this juncture certain key words have emerged. Almost too many. The first—the one with which I began—is "unlosable." In this case, the unlosable that has proven itself to be entirely losable. And about which, ever since, one knew to be revocable. "Fatherland"? I would rather speak of Motherland, the land of my origin, the land of my language.

"Fatherland," as a distinguished scholar of linguistics recently said, is "a translation from Latin. The word may well be forgotten given the way it has been discredited." Motherland: this once referred to a metropolis, seen from the viewpoint of a colony. One no longer thinks of this when using this word. At least I do not. And I have tried this out with others, none of whom made this connection. The land of one's birth. Mother-tongue [*Muttersprache*]. "The mother-tongue is the speech of one's mother as long as one's mother speaks the language of her surroundings [*die Sprache des Ambientes*]," this linguist said to me. But this is the way things normally are. The mother-tongue is the language of childhood.

For me, language is what is unlosable once everything else has proven to be otherwise. It is the last irrevocable home. Only the death of the person, when the brain ceases to function, can take this from us. For me, this means the German language. For in other languages that I speak I remain a guest. Happily and gratefully so, but still a guest. The German language provided stability, and we have it to thank for the fact that we could safeguard our very identity. Because of this language I returned from exile to Germany.

It was one of the great excitements of my life finally to return home [after the war]. To the land of my birth where people speak German. Perhaps, or rather certainly, this was much more exciting than my leaving [in 1932], in those times. In between was the time of exile, the "not-belonging-to" [*das Nicht-Dazugehören*], an experience one can only realize in a piecemeal manner since one does not see this in its entirety ahead of time. Only in going forth does one recognize how unsettling this new circumstance is, and how sinister [*un-heimlich*].

When I see images of those who are fleeing on the news, all who find themselves setting out on a trek, all those hanging onto planes in the hope of getting to some new destination, I already know how questionable the arrival will be and do not have to wait for another week or month to receive the next report.

I have experienced this myself, this "permanent flight." And I had the good fortune to escape being captured when I had run far enough, I was even allowed to return from the edge of the world. And go home.

"You speak of homeland," Hans Magnus Enzensberger said to me in the early 1950s. "For this you crossed over the seas to tell us this, when in fact it was all just a question of the backdrop."

It appeared to him, in other words, that the backdrop had also transformed itself for those who had remained at home.

This "being at-home" [*Zuhausesein*], this "being-allowed-to-belong" [*Hingehörendürfen*], though, is not simply a question of the scenery. Nor is it merely a matter of well-being. It means to take on shared responsible [*mitverantwortlich zu sein*]. Not just to be a foreigner. To be able, when necessary, to interfere oneself. To claim the right to have one's say, which is our birthright.

In this context, the loss of the sense of belonging is a wounding that never fully scars over. "Home [*das Zuhause*] should not have to be painful, like a backache or a cavity." But it is painful in every situation. And these situations have increased in recent years. The exemplary expulsion like that of the grandparents' generation: through this one learns everything, literally everything, about being human, and about what it means to be a "fugitive-guest" ["*einflüchtiger-Gast-sein*"] This, then, is not a metaphor one might hear spoken from the pulpit.

As with the experience of home, so also with love, as soon as one has learned that this might be withdrawn. For love has become almost as much tabued as homeland. Those who are "in" speak only of sex. But this, too, has changed: love has now become socially accepted. Even homeland [*Heimat*] is under discussion. (It has lost the hatred of militants that the associations of refugees had given it.) In earlier times, at best, this pertained to people like Ernst Bloch, Nelly Sachs, and me. Now it has become a pressing matter. For we live in a crisis affecting forms of belonging [*eine Krise der Zugehörigkeiten*]. Also in a language-crisis and one related to our ways of speaking. The communication-crisis, the identity-crisis. In the "not-homeland" [*in der Nicht-Heimat*]. Such concepts are often dealt with superficially, as if they were a game of balls. Those who have truly experienced this, who have been traumatized by it, resist this. The language by which I conscientiously name the world, and by which, conscientiously, I render it communicable (and do this such that I will be heard), this cannot be taken away; it is our final refuge. I will defend this home [*dieses Zuhause*] to my last breath. Just as a farmer once protected his farmland. I can do no other than this.

Everything that I defend, where I make my stand, is not on this side of doubt but beyond it. The apple of knowledge has been shoved down our throats, and this cannot be reversed. As H. A. P. Grieshaber wrote to me shortly before his death, "What good would it be if we were forty years old now and did not have this wound!" If only we could vaccinate the younger generation with our tears.

The Wandering Radiance

Selected Poems of
Hilde Domin

NICHT MÜDE WERDEN

Nicht müde werden
sondern dem Wunder
leise
wie einem Vogel
die Hand hinhalten.

Don't Grow Weary

Don't grow weary
but hold your hand out
quietly
to the miracle
as if to a bird.

ZWISCHEN IMMER UND IMMER

Leuchtend sanfte
Fläche des Herzens,
Stille
ausgespannt
—wie zwischen immer und immer—
zwischen Morgen und Abend
von Bucht zu Bucht

Das Boot mit dem weißen Segel
macht keinen Einschnitt
auf dem Blau deiner Milch
Das schnellere Weiß der Möwe
das den Atem mitnimmt
in weiten Schleifen
läßt keine Spur

Aber der wandernde Glanz
die große langsame Hand die
unerbittlich liebkosend
dir über das ewige Herz streicht
hält nicht ein
und schiebt die Stunden weg
auf dem Zifferblatt deiner Küsten

Mit ihrem Zeigefinger aus Schatten und Gold
weist sie die Vögel ins Schweigen
in dem breiten Palmkorb der Nacht
und tilgt das Geschenk dieses Tags
aus dem zärtlich kurzen
Blüten-urlaub
der leichten Mimosen

BETWEEN ALWAYS AND ALWAYS

Shining soft
surface of the heart,
stillness
stretched out
—as between always and always—
between morning and evening
from cove to cove

The boat with the white sail
doesn't cut into
the blue of your milk
The gull's quicker white
that carries breath with it
in wide loops
leaves no trace behind

But the wandering radiance
the large slow hand that
unrelentingly caressing
strokes you above the eternal heart
doesn't pause
and pushes the hours away
on the clockface of your shoreline

With her index finger made of shadow and gold
she signals the birds to keep silent
in the wide palm-basket of the night
and redeems the gift of this day
from the tender short
blossom-holiday
of the gentle mimosas

INDISCHER FALTER

Vielleicht sind wir nichts als
Schalen
womit der Augenblick
geschöpft wird.

In einem alten Mann
der umfällt in Hamburg oder Manhattan
stirbt ein Schmetterling
die blauen Flügel öffnend
—seit dreißig Jahren,
in Angkor-Vath.

Vielleicht wird nichts verlangt
von uns
während wir hier sind,
als ein Gesicht
leuchten zu machen
bis es durchsichtig wird.

Und das Leuchten dieses einen Gesichts
aufzubewahren
wie der alte Mann
den Glanz seines indischen Falters.
Bis wir hingelegt werden
und alles für immer

erinnern—oder vergessen.

INDIAN LEAF BUTTERFLY

Perhaps we are nothing but
bowls
with which to scoop up
the moment.

In an old man
who collapses in Hamburg or Manhattan
a butterfly dies
opening its blue wings
—thirty years ago,
in Angkor-Vath.

Perhaps nothing else is asked
of us
while we are here
but to make a face
shine
until it becomes transparent.

And to protect the shining
of this one face
as the old man
protects the radiance of his Indian Leaf Butterfly.
Until we will be laid down
and remember everything

forever—or forget.

ANDERE GEBURT

Mutter dein Tod
ist unsere zweite Geburt
nackter hilfloser
als die erste

Weil du nicht da bist
und uns nicht in den Arm nimmst
um uns von uns selber
zu trösten

A Different Birth

Mother your death
is our second birth
more naked more helpless
than the first

Because you aren't here
and don't take us by the arm
to console us
from ourselves

Nur eine Rose als Stütze

Ich richte mir ein Zimmer ein in der Luft
unter den Akrobaten und Vögeln:
mein Bett auf dem Trapez des Gefühls
wie ein Nest im Wind
auf der äußersten Spitze des Zweigs.

Ich kaufe mir eine Decke aus der zartesten Wolle
der sanftgescheitelten Schafe die
im Mondlicht
wie schimmernde Wolken
über die feste Erde ziehn.

Ich schließe die Augen und hülle mich ein
in das Vlies der verläßlichen Tiere.
Ich will den Sand unter den kleinen Hufen spüren
und das Klicken des Riegels hören,
der die Stalltür am Abend schließt.

Aber ich liege in Vogelfedern, hoch ins Leere gewiegt.
Mir schwindelt. Ich schlafe nicht ein.
Meine Hand
greift nach einem Halt und findet
nur eine Rose als Stütze.

Only a Rose for Support

I furnish a room in the air
among acrobats and birds:
my bed on the trapeze of feeling
like a nest in the wind
on the branches' outermost tips.

I buy a blanket made of the softest wool
from the gentle-headed sheep that
wander
in moonlight
like shimmering clouds
above the solid earth.

I close my eyes and wrap myself
in the fleece of these dependable animals.
I want to feel the sand beneath their small hoofs
and hear the click of the latch
that locks the stable door in the evening.

But I lie in bird-feathers, cradled high in the void.
I'm dizzy. I don't fall asleep.
My hand
reaches for a firm hold and finds
only a rose for support.

Landen dürfen

Ich nannte mich
ich selber rief mich
mit dem Namen einer Insel.

Es ist der Name eines Sonntags
einer geträumten Insel.
Kolumbus erfand die Insel
an einem Weihnachtssonntag.

Sie war eine Küste
etwas zum Landen
man kann sie betreten
die Nachtigallen singen an Weihnachten dort.

Nennen Sie sich, sagte einer
als ich in Europa an Land ging,
mit dem Namen Ihrer Insel.

ALLOWED TO LAND

I named myself
I personally called myself
by the name of an island.

It is the name of a Sunday
of a dreamt-of island.
Columbus discovered the island
on a Christmas Sunday.

It was a coastline
a place to land
one could step onto it
the nightingales sing there on Christmas.

Name yourself, someone said to me
as I went ashore in Europe,
with the name of your island.

ZIEHENDE LANDSCHAFT

Man muß weggehen können
und doch sein wie ein Baum:
als bliebe die Wurzel im Boden,
als zöge die Landschaft und wir ständen fest.
Man muß den Atem anhalten,
bis der Wind nachläßt
und die fremde Luft um uns zu kreisen beginnt,
bis das Spiel von Licht und Schatten,
von Grün und Blau,
die alten Muster zeigt
und wir zuhause sind,
wo es auch sei,
und niedersitzen können und uns anlehnen,
als sei es an das Grab
unserer Mutter.

PULLING LANDSCAPE

One must be able to depart
and yet remain like a tree:
as if the roots remained in the ground,
as if the landscape pulled and we stood still.
One must hold one's breath
until the wind abates
and the strange air around us begins to stir,
until the game of light and shadows,
green and blue,
shows its old pattern
and we find ourselves at home
wherever that might be,
and can sit down and lean back
against the grave
of our mother.

Lyrik

das Nichtwort

ausgespannt
zwischen

Wort und Wort.

Poetry

the not-word

stretched out
between

word and word.

NOTRUFER

In mir ist immer
Abschied:
Wie ein Ertrinkender
dessen Kleider
von Meerwasser schwer sind
seine letzte Liebe
einer kleinen Wolke schenkt.

In mir ist immer
Glaube,
als sei das goldene Seil
wer es auch auswirft
dem Notrufer
heilig
geschuldet.

EMERGENCY-CALLER

Departure
is always within me:
Like one who is drowning
whose clothes
are heavy with saltwater
who gives his last love
to a little cloud.

Faith
is always within me,
as if the golden cord
whoever throws it forth
were sacredly
owed to
the emergency-caller.

WO STEHT UNSER MANDELBAUM

Ich liege
in deinen Armen, Liebster,
wie der Mandelkern in der Mandel.
Sag mir: wo steht
unser Mandelbaum?

Ich liege in deinen Armen
wie in einem Schiff,
ohne Route noch Hafen,
aber mit Delphinen am Bug.

Unter unserem Rücken
ein Band von Betten,
unsere Betten in den vielen Ländern,
im Nirgendwo der Nacht,
wenn rings ein fremdes Zimmer versinkt.

Wohin wir kamen
—wohin wir kommen, Liebster,
alles ist anders,
alles ist gleich.

Überall wird das Heu
auf andere Weise geschichtet
zum Trocknen
unter der gleichen
Sonne.

WHERE IS OUR ALMOND TREE

I lie
in your arms, darling,
like the almond kernel in its shell.
Tell me: Where is
our almond tree?

I lie in your arms
as if in a ship
without a route or harbor,
but with dolphins at the bow.

Beneath our backs
a cord of beds,
our beds in many lands,
in the nowhere of the night,
when all around a strange room sinks down.

Wherever we came to
—wherever we come to, darling,
everything's different,
everything's the same.

Everywhere hay is
stacked differently
to dry
under the same
sun.

Im Regen geschrieben

Wer wie die Biene wäre,
die die Sonne
auch durch den Wolkenhimmel fühlt,
die den Weg zur Blüte findet
und nie die Richtung verliert,
dem lägen die Felder in ewigem Glanz,
wie kurz er auch lebte,
er würde selten
weinen.

Written in the Rain

Whoever would be like the bee
who feels the sun
even through a cloudy sky,
who finds the way to the blossoms
and never loses track of the direction,
for such a one the fields would lie in eternal radiance,
no matter how briefly he were to live,
and seldom would he
weep.

ES KOMMEN KEINE NACH UNS

Es kommen keine nach uns,
die es erzählen werden,
keine, die was wir
ungetan ließen,
in die Hand nehmen und zu Ende tun.

Wir stehen auf einem Stück Land,
das schon abgetrennt ist.
Unsere Schatten fallen
ins Leere.
Kein Spiegel ist aufgestellt,
der unser Bild bewahrt,
keine Folge von Spiegeln mehr,
wenn wir gegangen sind.
Die Bilder
derer, die vor uns waren
und die Luft in unserer Lunge sind,
die mit unserem Munde gelacht,
die mit unseren Augen geweint haben,
sie werden Staub
mit uns.

So wie wir dahingehn
sind wenige dahingegangen.
Es ist gleichgültig
was wir schreiben oder sagen,
außer für dich oder für mich.
Nichts was wir tun
ist eine Saat die nach uns aufgeht.
Wir sind ganz für den Tag gemacht,
nur für diesen, den unsern.

None Come After Us

None come after us
to explain it,
none to take into their hands
what we left undone,
and complete it.

We stand on a piece of land
that has already been cut off.
Our shadows fall
into the abyss.
No mirror is set out
to protect our image,
no series of mirrors remains
when we're gone.
The images
of those who lived before us
and are the air in our lungs,
who laughed with our mouth,
who wept with our eyes,
they will become dust
with us.

Where those like us go
few have gone.
It doesn't matter
what we write or say,
except for you or for me.
Nothing we do
is a seed that will sprout when we're gone.
We're made entirely for the day,
only for this day, our day.

Die kommenden Tage,
die Tage hinter dem Horizont,
gehören Menschen die anders sein werden.
Unser Frühling ist dieser Frühling,
unser Sommer ist dieser Sommer,
und unser Herbst dieser Herbst.

Wenn wir uns umdrehn
und sehen, daß wir die Letzten sind,
die Kinder und Kindeskinder derer die waren,
die Väter und Mütter
von niemand,
daß wir am Rande stehn,
auf einer Scholle fast,
die bald treiben wird,

Dann müssen wir
mehr als die andern
den Boden unter den Füßen fühlen
während wir gehen,
diesen kurzen Boden
von Morgen zu Abend.
Wir müssen dünne Sohlen tragen
oder barfuß gehen.
Was wir berühren,
mit leichtem Finger berühren,
mit wachen Fingerspitzen.
Nichts achtlos.

Jedes Mal ist das letzte
oder könnte es sein.
Wir tun es für alle, die vor uns waren,
und für alle, die nach uns
es nicht tun
oder ganz anders.

The coming days,
the days beyond the horizon,
belong to those who will become different.
Our spring is this spring,
our summer is this summer,
and our fall this fall.

When we turn around
and see that we're the last ones,
the children and grandchildren of those who were,
the fathers and mothers
of no one,
that we stand at the edge,
as if on an icefloe
that will soon begin to move,

Then we must feel
more strongly than the others
the ground beneath our feet
as we go,
this bit of ground
from morning until evening.
We must wear thin soles
or go barefoot.
What we touch,
with light finger touch,
with wakeful fingertips.
Nothing carelessly.

Each time is the last
or could be.
We do this for all who were before us,
and for all those after us
who won't do it
or will do it completely differently.

Wir wollen nichts liegen lassen,
halbgetan,
und die Gläser nicht halbgeleert
auf unserm Tisch den Gespenstern lassen.
Wir müssen genau sein
in der Minute des Flügelschlags.
Unser Gesicht nackt
ohne den Firnis
derer, die Zeit haben
sich zu gewöhnen und zu entwöhnen.
Wenn um unsre Balkone das Wasser steigt,
die Spitzen der Bäume
noch sichtbar unter den Sternen,
wenn unsre Häuser auf den Bergen,
in denen noch Licht ist,
sich bewegen
und davonfahrn
als seien es Archen,
dann müssen wir bereit sein
—wie einer der aus dem Fenster springt—
die große Frage zu fragen
und die große Antwort zu hören.

We want to leave nothing undone,
half-done,
don't want to leave the glasses half-emptied
on our table for the ghosts.
We must be precise
in the minute of the wing-beat.
Our face naked
without the varnish
of those who have time
to get used to it and to wean themselves from it.
When the water rises up to our balconies,
the treetops
still visible beneath the stars,
when our houses on the mountains
in which there is still light
stir themselves
and depart
as if they were arks,
then we must be ready
—like one who springs from the window—
to ask the great questions
and to hear the great answers.

APPELL

1
Geh nicht als ein Erlöschender
Geh nicht als ein Erlöschender
Geh nicht als ein Erlöschender
in das Erlöschen

Brenne
Brenne
Wir sind Fackeln mein Bruder
Wir sind Sterne
Wir sind Brennendes
Steigendes
Oder wir sind nicht
gewesen

2
Ein Körper
wie der unsere
ist nur die Hülle des Ballons
lichtdurchlässig

APPEAL[1]

1
Don't go as one burning out
Don't go as one burning out
Don't go as one burning out
into the extinction

Burn
Burn
We are torches my brother
We are stars
We are something burning
Something rising
Or we've not
been at all

2
A body
like ours
is only the sheathing of the balloon
penetrable by light

ABEL STEH AUF

Abel steh auf
es muß neu gespielt werden
täglich muß es neu gespielt werden
täglich muß die Antwort noch vor uns sein
die Antwort muß ja sein können
wenn du nicht aufstehst Abel
wie soll die Antwort
diese einzig wichtige Antwort
sich je verändern
wir können alle Kirchen schließen
und alle Gesetzbücher abschaffen
in allen Sprachen der Erde
wenn du nur aufstehst
und es rückgängig machst
die erste falsche Antwort
auf die einzige Frage
auf die es ankommt
steh auf
damit Kain sagt
damit er es sagen kann
Ich bin dein Hüter
Bruder
wie sollte ich nicht dein Hüter sein
Täglich steh auf
damit wir es vor uns haben
dies Ja ich bin hier
ich
dein Bruder

ABEL GET UP

Abel get up
it must be done again
every day it must be done again
every day the answer must be before us
the answer yes must be possible
if you don't get up Abel
how should the answer
this answer which is the only important one
ever change
we could close all the churches
and do away with all the law books
in all the languages of the earth
if you would only get up
and reverse this
the first wrong answer
to the only question
that matters
get up
so that Cain says
so that he can say
I am your keeper
brother
how could I not be your keeper
Get up every day
so that we have this before us
this Yes I am here
I
your brother

Damit die Kinder Abels
sich nicht mehr fürchten
weil Kain nicht Kain wird
Ich schreibe dies
ich ein Kind Abels
und fürchte mich täglich
vor der Antwort
die Luft in meiner Lunge wird weniger
wie ich auf die Antwort warte

Abel steh auf
damit es anders anfängt
zwischen uns allen

Die Feuer die brennen
das Feuer das brennt auf der Erde
soll das Feuer von Abel sein

Und am Schwanz der Raketen
sollen die Feuer von Abel sein

So that Abel's children
won't be afraid any longer
because Cain won't be Cain
I write this
I a child of Abel
and I fear the answer
every day
the air in my lungs diminishes
as I wait for the answer

Abel get up
so that it can begin differently
between us all

The fires that burn
the fire that burns upon the earth
should be Abel's fire

And the tail of the rocket
should be Abel's fire

GRAUE ZEITEN

1

Es muß aufgehoben werden
als komme es aus grauen Zeiten

Menschen wie wir wir unter ihnen
fuhren auf Schiffen hin und her
und konnten nirgends landen

Menschen wie wir wir unter ihnen
durften nicht bleiben
und konnten nicht gehen

Menschen wie wir wir unter ihnen
grüßten unsere Freunde nicht
und wurden nicht gegrüßt

Menschen wie wir wir unter ihnen
standen an fremden Küsten
um Verzeihung bittend daß es uns gab

Menschen wie wir wir unter ihnen
wurden bewahrt

Menschen wie wir wir unter ihnen
Menschen wie ihr ihr unter ihnen
jeder

kann ausgezogen werden
und nackt gemacht
die nackten Menschenpuppen

Gray Times[2]

1
It must be lifted up
as if it came from gray times

People like us us among them
rode in ships back and forth
And could land nowhere

People like us us among them
were not allowed to stay
and could not leave

People like us us among them
did not greet our friends
and were not greeted

People like us us among them
stood on foreign coasts
pleading for forgiveness that we existed

People like us us among them
were spared

People like us us among them
People like you you among them
anyone

can be undressed
and stripped naked
the naked human puppets

nackter als Tierleiber
unter den Kleidern
der Leib der Opfer

Ausgezogen
die noch morgens die Schalen um sich haben
weiße Körper

Glück hatte wer nur
gestoßen wurde
von Pol zu Pol

Die grauen Zeiten
Montag viel Dienstags nichts
zwischen

uns und den grauen Zeiten

2
Die grauen Zeiten
von denen nichts uns trennt als
zwanzig Jahre

Die Köpfe der Zeitungen
das Rot und das Schwarz
unter dem Worte ‚Deutsch'

ich sah es schon einmal
Zwanzig Jahre:

Montag viel Dienstag nichts
zwischen

uns und den grauen Zeiten

more naked than animals' bodies
beneath the clothing
the body of victims

Undressed
those who still in the morning had shells around themselves
white bodies

Those were lucky who were only
shoved about
from pole to pole

The gray times
Monday many Tuesdays nothing
between

us and the gray times

2
The gray times
from which nothing but twenty years
separated us

Newspaper banners
the red and the black
beneath the word "German"

I saw it once already
Twenty years:

Monday and often Tuesday nothing
between

us and the gray times

3
Manchmal sehe ich dich

von wilden Tieren zerrissen
von Menschentieren

Wir lachen vielleicht

Deine Angst die ich nie sah
diese Angst
ich sehe euch

4
Dich
und den
und den
Menschen wie ihr
ihr unter ihnen
Menschen wie wir
wir unter ihnen
Nackte Menschenpuppen
die heute noch die Schalen um sich haben

Die Köpfe der Zeitungen
das Rot und das Schwarz
unter dem Worte ‚Deutsch‘
Die Toten stehen neben den Kiosken
und sehen mit großen Augen
die Köpfe der Zeitungen an
den schwarz und rot gedruckten Haß
unter dem Worte ‚Deutsch‘
Die Toten fürchten sich

Dies ist ein Land
in dem die Toten sich fürchten

3
Sometimes I see you

torn apart by wild animals
by animal-people

We laugh perhaps

Your fear which I never saw
this fear
I see you all

4
You
and that one
and that one
one like you
you among them
People like us
us among them
Naked human puppets
who still today have scarves wrapped around them

Newspaper banners
the red and the black
beneath the word "German"
The dead stand next to the kiosks
and stare with eyes wide open
at the newspaper banners
at the black- and the red-printed hate
beneath the word "German"
The dead are afraid

This is a nation
in which the dead are afraid

VATERLÄNDER

Soviel Vaterländer wie der Mensch hat
vaterlandslos
heimatlos
jede neue Vertreibung
ein neues Land macht die Arme auf
mehr oder weniger
die Arme der Paßkontrolle
und dann die Menschen
immer sind welche da
die Arme öffnen
eine Gymnastik
in diesem Jahrhundert
der Füße der Arme
unordentlicher Gebrauch unserer Glieder
irgend etwas ist immer da
das sich zu lieben lohnt
irgend etwas ist nie da

Alle diese Länder haben Grenzen
gegen Nachbarländer

FATHERLANDS

As many fatherlands as one has
fatherlandless
homelandless
each new expulsion
a new land opens its arms
more or less
the arms of the immigration officers
and then the people
always there are some there
who open their arms
a gymnastic move
in this century
of feet of arms
a disorderly use of our limbs
something is always there
that is worth loving
something is never there

All these countries have borders
against neighboring lands

LOSGELÖST

Losgelöst
treibt ein Wort

auf dem Wasser der Zeit
und dreht sich
und wird getragen
oder geht unter.

Du hast mich lange vergessen.
Ich erinnre schon niemand,
dich nicht
und niemand.

Dies Wort von mir zu dir,
dies treibende Blatt,
es könnte von jedem
Baum

auf das Wasser gefallen sein.

Released

Freed
a word does its work

on the water of time
and turns
and is carried
or goes under.

You've long forgotten me.
I'm not reminding anyone,
not you
and no one.

This word from me to you,
this drifting leaf,
it could have fallen from any
tree

onto the water.

MIT MEINEM SCHATTEN

Ich gehe mit meinem Schatten,
nur von dem Schatten begleitet,
alleine mit ihm,
über graslose Wiesen.

Ich immer blässer,
er immer länger.
Er führt mich,
ich lasse mich führen.

Die kahlen Birken am Weg,
glatte weiße Finger,
kennen das Ziel
besser als ich.

WITH MY SHADOW

I walk with my shadow,
accompanied only by my shadow,
alone with it,
across grassless meadows.

I ever paler,
my shadow ever longer.
It leads me,
I let myself be led.

The bare birches along the way,
smooth white fingers,
know the destination
better than I.

Wie wenig ich nütze bin

Wie wenig nütze ich bin,
ich hebe den Finger und hinterlasse
nicht den kleinsten Strich
in der Luft.

Die Zeit verwischt mein Gesicht,
sie hat schon begonnen.
Hinter meinen Schritten im Staub
wäscht Regen die Straße blank
wie eine Hausfrau.

Ich war hier.
Ich gehe vorüber
ohne Spur.
Die Ulmen am Weg
winken mir zu wie ich komme,
grün blau goldener Gruß,
und vergessen mich,
eh ich vorbei bin.

Ich gehe vorüber—
aber ich lasse vielleicht
den kleinen Ton meiner Stimme,
mein Lachen und meine Tränen
und auch den Gruß der Bäume im Abend
auf einem Stückchen Papier.

Und im Vorbeigehn,
ganz absichtslos,
zünde ich die ein oder andere
Laterne an
in den Herzen am Wegrand.

However Little Use I Am

However little use I am,
I lift a finger and leave behind
not even the smallest stroke
in the air.

Time smudges my face,
it has already begun.
Behind my steps in the dust
rain washes the street clean
like a housewife.

I was here.
I cross over
without a trace.
The elms along the way
nod to me as I come,
a green a blue a golden greeting,
and forget me
before I've passed by.

I cross over—
but leave perhaps
the small sound of my voice,
my laughter and my tears
and also the trees' greeting in the evening
on a small scrap of paper.

And in passing,
entirely without intention,
I light one or another
of the streetlamps
in the hearts along the roadside.

VOR TAG

Der Kuß aus Rosenblättern,
immer neue weiche kleine
Blätter der sich öffnenden Blüte.

Nicht jenes Wenig von Raum
für die Spanne des Wunschs
zwischen Nehmen und Geben.

Du hobst die Decke von mir
so behutsam
wie man ein Kind nicht weckt
oder als wär ich
so zerbrechlich
wie ich bin.

Ich wurde nicht wirklicher
als ein Gedicht
oder ein Traum
oder die Wolke
unter der Wolke.

Und doch, als du fort warst,
der zärtliche Zweifel:
Ist es tröstlich
für einen Mann
mit einer Wolke zu schlafen?

BEFORE DAY BEGINS

The kiss of rose petals,
always new soft little
leaves of the opening blossom.

Not that little bit of room
for the span of wishes
between taking and giving.

You lifted the blanket from me
as carefully
as one does not to wake a child
or as if I were
as fragile
as I am.

I did not become more real
than a poem
or a dream
or a cloud
beneath a cloud.

And yet, after you'd gone,
the tender doubt:
Is it comforting
for a man
to sleep with a cloud?

EXIL

Meinem Vater

Der sterbende Mund
müht sich
um das richtig gesprochene
Wort
einer fremden
Sprache.

EXILE

For my Father

The dying mouth
struggles
to find the rightly spoken
word
in a foreign
tongue.

HERBSTZEITLOSEN

Für uns, denen der Pfosten der Tür verbrannt ist,
an dem die Jahre der Kindheit
Zentimeter für Zentimeter
eingetragen waren.

Die wir keinen Baum
in unseren Garten pflanzten,
um den Stuhl
in seinen wachsenden Schatten zu stellen.

Die wir am Hügel niedersitzen,
als seien wir zu Hirten bestellt
der Wolkenschafe, die auf der blauen
Weide über den Ulmen dahinziehn.

Für uns, die stets unterwegs sind
—lebenslängliche Reise,
wie zwischen Planeten—
nach einem neuen Beginn.

Für uns
stehen die Herbstzeitlosen auf
in den braunen Wiesen des Sommers,
und der Wald füllt sich
mit Brombeeren und Hagebutten—

Damit wir in den Spiegel sehen
und es lernen
unser Gesicht zu lesen,
in dem die Ankunft
sich langsam entblößt.

AUTUMN CROCUS

For us, for whom the doorjamb is burned
on which the years of childhood
were recorded,
centimeter by centimeter.

We who planted
no trees in our garden
to place a chair
in its growing shade.

We who reclined on the hill
as if appointed as shepherds
for the cloud-sheep that roll along
over the blue meadow above the elms.

For us who are always on the way
—a lifelong trip,
as if among the planets—
toward a new beginning.

For us
the autumn crocus rise up
in the brown fields of summer,
and the forest fills itself
with blackberries and rosehips—

So that we might look in the mirror
and learn to read
our face,
in which the arrival
slowly reveals itself.

RÜCKKEHR DER SCHIFFE

Du hast alles fortgehen lassen
was dir gehörte.
Auch die Erwartung.
Abgewandt stieg sie aufs Schiff,
ehe sich's löste
aus deiner Bucht.

Du vergißt dein Gesicht.
Ein Toter fast
der sich noch regt
und der sich noch die Nägel schneiden kann,
dem auch die Wangen oft naß sind,
ohne daß er merkt daß er weint.

Aber nichts stirbt ganz.
Schläft nur in dir, dem fast Toten.
Alles kann wiederkommen.
Nicht so.
Aber doch, auf seine Art,
wieder-kommen.

Auch das Schiff.
Alle deine Schiffe zugleich.
Ein sanftes Licht.
Du weißt es selber nicht,
sind dir die Schiffe heimgekehrt,
heben hohe Bäume sich aus dir?

Nur daß Weite und Licht ist
in deiner unendlichen Brust
und sich alles versöhnt, bei seiner
Einfahrt in diese große Wunde
ohne Ränder, die
vollsteht mit einem süßen Wasser.

RETURN OF THE SHIPS

You let everything leave
that belonged to you.
Even the expectations.
Having turned away, they boarded the ship
before it set out
from your harbor.

You forget your face.
One almost dead
who can still move
and can still clip his nails,
whose cheeks are often moist
without his noticing that he cried.

But nothing dies entirely.
It merely sleeps in you who're almost dead.
Everything can come again.
Not this way.
And yet in its own manner,
coming-again.

Even the ship.
All your ships at once.
A soft light.
You don't know it yourself—
have the ships returned home to you,
have tall trees hoisted themselves from within you?

Only that breadth and light is
in your unending chest
and everything is reconciled in its
entry into this great edgeless
wound,
filled to the brim with a sweet water.

KÖLN

Die versunkene Stadt
für mich
allein
versunken.

Ich schwimme
in diesen Straßen.
Andere gehn.

Die alten Häuser
haben neue große Türen
aus Glas.

Die Toten und ich
wir schwimmen
durch die neuen Türen
unserer alten Häuser.

Cologne

The sunken city
for me
alone
sunken.

I swim
in these streets.
Others walk.

The old houses
have large new doors
made of glass.

The dead and I
we swim
through the new doors
of our old houses.

Ich will dich

Freiheit
ich will dich
aufrauhen mit Schmirgelpapier
du geleckte

die ich meine
meine
unsere
Freiheit von und zu
Modefratz

Du wirst geleckt
mit Zungenspitzen
bis du ganz rund bist
Kugel
auf allen Tüchern

Freiheit Wort
das ich aufrauhen will
ich will dich mit Glassplittern spicken
daß man dich schwer auf die Zunge nimmt
und du niemandes Ball bist

Dich
und andere
Worte möchte ich mit Glassplittern spicken
wie es Konfuzius befiehlt
der alte Chinese

Die Eckenschale sagt er
muß
Ecken haben
sagt er
Oder der Staat geht zugrunde

I Want You

Freedom
I want you
roughed up with sandpaper
you licked one

which I mean
my
our
Freedom
turned-fashion-brat-nobility

You're licked
with tips of tongues
until you're entirely round
a sphere
on all scarves

Freedom word
that I want to rough up
I want to spike glass splinters into you
so that it'll be hard to take you on the tongue
and you'll be no one's ball

You
and other
words I want to spike with glass splinters
as Confucius ordered
that old Chinese sage

The square bowl
must be square
he said
Or the country will go to ruin

Nichts weiter sagt er
ist vonnöten
Nennt
das Runde rund
und das Eckige eckig

Nothing more he said
is needed
Call
what is round round
and what is square square

BITTERSÜSSER MANDELBAUM

Die Zweige müssen die Blüten verlieren,
damit die Bäume grünen:
das Rosa und das Weiß
der süßen und bitteren Mandel
mischt sich am Boden.

War das Süße ins Bittre
oder das Bittre ins Süße gepfropft?
Alle Blüten sind voller Honig,
leichte Schmetterlingswiegen,
alles Blühen ist süß.

Doch wenn erst das Laub
die doppelte Krone vereint,
unter dem blauesten Himmel,
im sanftesten Wind,
wird dann das Bittere bitter.

Bittersweet Almond Tree

The branches must lose their blossoms
so that the trees can green:
the pink and the white
of the sweet and bitter almond
mingle on the ground below.

Was the sweet grafted into the bitter
or the bitter into the sweet?
All the blossoms are full of honey,
light butterfly-cradles,
all blossoming is sweet.

But when the foliage first
joins the doubled crown,
under the bluest skies,
in the softest wind,
that's when the bitter becomes bitter.

WER ES KÖNNTE

Wer es könnte
die Welt
hochwerfen
daß der Wind
hindurchfährt.

Who Could Do It

Who could do it
throw the world
so high
that the wind
could pass through it.

UNTERRICHT

Jeder der geht
belehrt uns ein wenig
über uns selber.
Kostbarster Unterricht
an den Sterbebetten.
Alle Spiegel so klar
wie ein See nach großem Regen,
ehe der dunstige Tag
die Bilder wieder verwischt.

Nur einmal sterben sie für uns,
nie wieder.
Was wüßten wir je
ohne sie?
Ohne die sicheren Waagen
auf die wir gelegt sind
wenn wir verlassen werden.
Diese Waagen ohne die nichts
sein Gewicht hat.

Wir, deren Worte sich verfehlen,
wir vergessen es.
Und sie?
Sie können die Lehre
nicht wiederholen.

Dein Tod oder meiner
der nächste Unterricht:
so hell, so deutlich,
daß es gleich dunkel wird.

INSTRUCTION

Everyone who leaves
teaches us a bit
about ourselves.
The most precious instruction
at the deathbed.
All the mirrors as clear
as a lake after heavy rain,
before the hazy day
blurs the images again.

Only once do they die for us,
never again.
What would we ever know
without them?
Without the reliable scales
that we're laid upon
when we have been abandoned.
These scales without which
nothing has weight.

We, whose words fail,
we forget it.
And they?
They can't repeat
their teaching.

Your death or mine
the next instruction:
so bright, so clear,
that it will soon become dark.

EIN GOLDENES BLATT

Ein goldenes Blatt
es schwebt auf mich zu
Ich wünsche nichts auf der Welt als das Blatt
Ich bleibe stehen
und mache die Hand auf
Ein leichter Wind
Das Blatt wird ein Schmetterling
Ich werde zum Jäger
Es fehlt mir das Netz
Ich müßte auf den Rasen laufen
um es zu fangen
Ich getraue mich nicht

Ich bitte das Blatt ich bitte den Wind
Ich tue einen kleinen Schritt
und halte die Hand hin
Das goldene Blatt
und meine Hand
verfehlen sich
wenig viel es ist gleich
Das Blatt ist ein gelbes
trockenes Blatt
eines der welken Blätter
im Gras
eines blauen Novembertags

A GOLDEN LEAF

A golden leaf
it drifts toward me
I want nothing more in this world than this leaf
I stand still
and hold out my hand
A gentle wind
The leaf becomes a butterfly
I become a hunter
But I'm without a net
I would have to run across the lawn
to catch it
I don't dare to

I ask the leaf I ask the wind
I take a small step
and hold out my hand
The golden leaf
and my hand
miss each other
by a little by a lot it's all the same
The leaf is a yellow
dried leaf
one of the withered leaves
in the grass
on a blue November day

Die schwersten Wege

Für R. H.

Die schwersten Wege
werden alleine gegangen,
die Enttäuschung, der Verlust,
das Opfer,
sind einsam.
Selbst der Tote der jedem Ruf antwortet
und sich keiner Bitte versagt
steht uns nicht bei
und sieht zu
ob wir es vermögen.
Die Hände der Lebenden die sich ausstrecken
ohne uns zu erreichen
sind wie die Äste der Bäume im Winter.
Alle Vögel schweigen.
Man hört nur den eigenen Schritt
und den Schritt den der Fuß
noch nicht gegangen ist aber gehen wird.
Stehenbleiben und sich Umdrehn
hilft nicht. Es muß
gegangen sein.

Nimm eine Kerze in die Hand
wie in den Katakomben,
das kleine Licht atmet kaum.
Und doch, wenn du lange gegangen bist,
bleibt das Wunder nicht aus,
weil das Wunder immer geschieht,
und weil wir ohne die Gnade
nicht leben können:
die Kerze wird hell vom freien Atem des Tags,
du bläst sie lächelnd aus

The Hardest Ways

For R. H.

The hardest ways
are walked alone;
disappointment, loss,
sacrifice,
are lonely.
Even the dead who answers every call
and refuses no request
doesn't stand with us
and watches to see
if we can handle it.
The hands of the living that stretch out
without reaching us
are like the branches of trees in winter.
The birds all keep still.
One hears only one's own footstep,
and the step one's foot
has not yet walked but will.
Remaining where we are and turning around
doesn't help. It's necessary
to go.

Take a candle in hand
as in the catacombs,
the little light scarcely breathes.
And yet after going a long way,
the miracle won't fail to appear,
because the miracle is always happening,
and because we cannot live
without grace:
the candle brightens with the day's unencumbered breath,
you blow it out laughing

wenn du in die Sonne trittst
und unter den blühenden Gärten
die Stadt vor dir liegt,
und in deinem Hause
dir der Tisch weiß gedeckt ist.
Und die verlierbaren Lebenden
und die unverlierbaren Toten
dir das Brot brechen und den Wein reichen—
und du ihre Stimmen wieder hörst
ganz nahe
bei deinem Herzen.

as you walk in the sun
and beneath the blooming garden
the city lies before you,
and in your house
where the table is bedecked with a white cloth for you.
And the living ones who can yet be lost
and the unlosable dead
break bread and serve wine—
and again you hear their voices
very close
to your heart.

AUF WOLKENBÜRGSCHAFT

Für Sabka

Ich habe Heimweh nach einem Land
in dem ich niemals war,
wo alle Bäume und Blumen
mich kennen,
in das ich niemals geh,
doch wo sich die Wolken
meiner
genau erinnern,
ein Fremder, der sich
in keinem Zuhause
ausweinen kann.

Ich fahre
nach Inseln ohne Hafen,
ich werfe die Schlüssel ins Meer
gleich bei der Ausfahrt.
Ich komme nirgends an.
Mein Segel ist wie ein Spinnweb im Wind,
aber es reißt nicht.
Und jenseits des Horizonts,
wo die großen Vögel
am Ende ihres Flugs
die Schwingen in der Sonne trocknen,
liegt ein Erdteil
wo sie mich aufnehmen müssen,
ohne Paß,
auf Wolkenbürgschaft.

On the Clouds' Guarantee

For Sabka

I am homesick for a land
where I've never been,
where all the trees and flowers
know me,
to which I'll never go,
but where the clouds
remember me
exactly,
a stranger who
has no home
in which to shed all their tears.

I travel
toward islands without harbors,
I throw the keys into the sea
as soon as I depart.
I arrive nowhere.
My sail is like a cobweb in the wind,
but it doesn't tear.
And beyond the horizon
where the great birds
dry their wings in the sun
at the end of their migration
there's a continent
where they must take me in
without a passport,
on the clouds' guarantee.

NIMM DEN EIMER

Nimm den Eimer
trage dich hin
Wisse du trägst dich
zu Dürstenden

Wisse du bist nicht das Wasser
du trägst nur den Eimer
Tränke sie dennoch

Dann trage den Eimer
voll mit dir
zu dir zurück

Der Gang
hin und her
dauert ein Jahrzehnt

(Du kannst es fünf- oder sechsmal tun
vom zwanzigsten Lebensjahr an gerechnet)

Take the Pail

Take the pail
carry yourself there
Know that you carry yourself
to those who thirst

Know that you're not the water
you only carry the pail
give them to drink nevertheless

Then carry the pail
filled with you
back to yourself

The way
there and back
lasts a decade

(You can do it five or six times
beginning when you're twenty)

KATALOG

Das Herz eine Schnecke
mit einem Haus
zieht die Hörner ein.

Das Herz ein Igel.

Das Herz eine Eule
bei Licht
mit den Augen klappernd.

Zugvogel Klimawechsler Herz.

Das Herz eine Kugel
gestoßen
einen Zentimeter rollend

Sandkorn Herz.

Das Herz der große
Werfer
aller Kugeln.

Catalog[3]

The heart a snail
with a house
draws in its horns.

The heart a hedgehog.

The heart an owl
in the light
with eyes blinking.

Migratory-bird changing-climate heart.

The heart a shot
put
a centimeter rolling

a grain-of-sand heart.

The heart the great
hurler
of all balls.

Magere Kost

Ich lege mich hin,
ich esse nicht und ich schlafe nicht,
ich gebe meinen Blumen
kein Wasser.
Es lohnt nicht den Finger zu heben.
Ich erwarte nichts.

Deine Stimme, die mich umarmt hat,
es ist viele Tage her,
ich habe jeden Tag
ein kleines Stück von ihr gegessen,
ich habe viele Tage
von ihr gelebt.
Bescheiden wie die Tiere der Armen
die am Wegrand
die schütteren Halme zupfen
und denen nichts gestreut wird.

So wenig, so viel
wie die Stimme,
die mich in den Arm nimmt,
mußt du mir lassen.
Ich atme nicht
ohne die Stimme.

Meager Fare

I lie down,
I don't eat and I don't sleep,
I don't water
my flowers.
It's not worth raising a finger.
I expect nothing.

Your voice which had embraced me,
that was days ago,
every day I've eaten
a little bit of it,
many days I've lived
from it.
As frugal as animals of the poor
that pluck the bare stalks
at the path's edge,
for whom nothing is scattered.

So little, so much
as the voice
that embraces me,
you must leave for me.
I don't breathe
without the voice.

LINGUISTIK

Du mußt mit dem Obstbaum reden.

Erfinde eine neue Sprache,
die Kirschblütensprache,
Apfelblütenworte,
rosa und weiße Worte,
die der Wind
lautlos
davonträgt.

Vertraue dich dem Obstbaum an
wenn dir ein Unrecht geschieht.
Lerne zu schweigen
in der rosa
und weißen Sprache.

Linguistics

You must speak with the fruit tree.

Discover a new language,
the cherry-blossom-language,
apple-blossom words,
pink and white words
that the wind carries
from them
silently.

Trust in the fruit free
whenever an injustice happens to you.
Learn to keep silent
in the pink
and white language.

RÜCKZUG

Ich bitte die Worte zu mir zurück
ich locke alle meine Worte
die hilflosen

Ich versammle die Bilder
die Landschaften kommen zu mir
die Bäume die Menschen

Nichts ist fern
alle versammeln sich
so viel Helle

Ich ein Teil von allem
kehre mit allem
in mich zurück
und verschließe mich
und gehe fort
aus der blühenden Helle
dem Grün dem Gold dem Blau
in das Erinnerungslose

RETREAT[4]

I call the words back to me
I lure all my words
the helpless ones

I gather the pictures
the landscapes come to me
the trees the people

Nothing is far
they all gather
so much brightness

I a part of them all
return with all of them
to myself
and close myself
and go forth
out of the blossoming brightness
out of the green the gold the blue
into memorylessness

LETZTE MITTEILUNG

Mein Bett ein Blatt
auf den Gefällen der Nächte,
immer schneller.

Ich sehe die Ufer nicht,
habe die Neugier verloren,
lege nicht an.

Das Segel aus Briefen
ziehe ich ein,
lasse keine Adresse.

Trost, spätfüßiger,
—gestern rief ich noch—
kann mich nie mehr erreichen.

LAST NOTICE

My bed a page
on the nights' slopes,
ever faster.

I don't see the shore,
have lost curiosity,
don't land.

I lower
the sail made of postal letters,
leave no address.

Solace, late-footed,
—yesterday I still called out—
can never again reach me.

VON UNS

Man wird in späteren Zeiten von uns lesen.

Nie wollte ich in späteren Zeiten
das Mitleid der Schulkinder erwecken.
Nie auf diese Art
in einem Schulheft stehn.

Wir, verurteilt
zu wissen
und nicht zu handeln.

Unser Staub
wird nie mehr Erde.

About Us

One will read about us in times to come.

I never wanted to arouse the sympathy
of schoolchildren in later times.
Never wanted to be mentioned
in a school lesson like this.

We, condemned
to know
and not to act.

Our dust
will never become earth again.

DIE LIEBE

Die Liebe
sitzt in der Sonne
auf einer Mauer und räkelt sich
für jeden zu sehn
Niemand hat sie gerufen
niemand könnte sie wegschicken
auch wenn sie störte

Woher kam sie als sie kam?
Man sieht selbst die Katze kommen
oder ein Gedicht auf dem Papier
Und der dunkelfüßige Traum
stellt sich nicht aus

Die Mauer ist leer
wo die Liebe saß
Wohin ging sie als sie ging?
Selbst der Tod, selbst die Träne
läßt eine Spur

LOVE

Love
sits in the sun
atop a wall and stretches out
for all to see
No one called her
no one could send her away
even if she were to disturb

Where did she come from when she came?
One sees even a cat coming
or a poem on paper
And the dark-footed dream
doesn't turn itself off

The wall is empty
where love sat
Where did she go when she went away?
Even death, even tears
leave a trail

Buchen im Frühling

Wir gehen zu zweit hinein
zu den Buchen im Frühling.
So silbern, so glatt, so dicht beieinander
die Stämme.
Das helle Laub wie Wolken am Himmel.
Du siehst hinauf und dir schwindelt.
Du entfernst dich ein wenig:
drei oder vier Bäume
zwischen uns.
Du verlierst dich
als sei ein Urteil gesprochen.
So nah, so getrennt.
Wir werden uns nie wieder
finden.

BEECHES IN SPRING

We enter together as a twosome
among the beeches in spring.
So silvery, so smooth, so close together
the trunks.
The bright leaves like clouds in the sky.
You look up and become dizzy.
You move away a little:
three or four trees
between us.
You lose yourself
as if a verdict were rendered.
So close, so separate.
We'll never find each other
again.

Neues Land

Es war leicht zu sein wie neues Land
wenn der Tag kam,
und nicht zu fragen
und die Stimme ins Blau zu schicken
wie eine Lerche.
Und wieder aufzustehn, wenn ich fiel,
ohne Narben.

Die Erde hat sich einmal zu oft gedreht.
Es hat nichts genutzt,
daß eine alte Frau
drei Gräser um meinen Fuß band,
als sei ich ein krankes Fohlen.
Ich bin aufgestanden
mit Narben.

Wenn du warten willst,
bis ich bin, wie ich war,
mußt du warten, bis ich sterbe.
Die Toten, sagt man, haben ein glattes Gesicht
und erfüllen uns jeglichen Wunsch.
Sie sind heiter
wie der Himmel im Frühling.

Und ohne zu fragen
und ohne verletzt zu sein,
sind sie immer
nur der Kern,
nie die Schale.

New Land

It was easy to be like new land
when the day came,
and not to ask
and to send the voice out into the blue
like a lark.
And to stand up again when I'd fallen,
without scars.

The earth has turned once too often.
It made no difference
that an old woman
bound three blades of grass around my foot
as if I were a sick foal.
I stood up
with scars.

If you want to wait
until I am as I was,
you'll have to wait until I die.
The dead, it is said, have a smooth face
and fulfill our every wish.
They're as cheerful
as the sky in spring.

And without asking
and without being wounded,
they're always
only the kernel,
never the shell.

FLUCHT

Es flieht das Herz
mit dem Mond,
die Wolken stehn,
der Mond hat Eile.

Es flieht der Mond,
das Herz hat Eile,
es reist den Träumen nach,
die Wolken stehn.

Die Träume häuten sich.
Es flieht das Herz

vor dem Gesicht
seines Traums.

FLIGHT

The heart flees
with the moon,
the clouds stand still,
the moon's in a hurry.

The moon flees,
the heart's in a hurry,
following dreams,
the clouds stand still.

Dreams shed their skin.
The heart flees

before the face
of its dreams.

AUSBRUCH VON HIER

Für Paul Celan, Péter Szondi, Jean Améry,
die nicht weiterleben wollten

Das Seil
nach Häftlingsart aus Bettüchern geknüpft
die Bettücher auf denen ich geweint habe
ich winde es um mich
Taucherseil
um meinen Leib
ich springe ab
ich tauche
weg vom Tag
hindurch
tauche ich auf
auf der andern Seite der Erde
Dort will ich
freier atmen
dort will ich ein Alphabet erfinden
von tätigen Buchstaben

ESCAPE FROM HERE

For Paul Celan, Peter Szondi, Jean Améry,
who didn't want to go on living[5]

The rope
made of bedsheets knotted the way prisoners do
the bed sheets on which I wept
I wind it around me
a diver's rope
around my body
I jump
dive
away from the day
all the way through
I surface
on the earth's other side
There I want to
breathe more freely
there I want to invent an alphabet
made of active letters

EIN BLAUER TAG

Ein blauer Tag
Nichts Böses kann dir kommen
an einem blauen Tag
Ein blauer Tag
die Kriegserklärung
Die Blumen öffneten ihr Nein
Die Vögel sangen Nein
ein König weinte
Niemand konnte es glauben
Ein blauer Tag
und doch war Krieg

Gestorben wird auch an blauen Tagen
bei jedem Wetter
Auch an blauen Tagen wirst du verlassen
und verläßt du
begnadigst nicht
und wirst nicht begnadigt
Auch an blauen Tagen
wird nichts zurückgenommen
Niemand kann es glauben:
Auch an blauen Tagen
bricht das Herz

A Blue Day

A blue day
Nothing bad can happen to you
on a blue day
A blue day
the declaration of war
The flowers opened their No
The birds sang No
a king cried
No one could believe it
A blue day
and still there was war

Dying occurs even on blue days
in every kind of weather
Even on blue days you'll be abandoned
and you abandon
refuse to pardon
and are not pardoned
Even on blue days
nothing is taken back
No one can believe it:
Even on blue days
the heart breaks

ZÄRTLICHE NACHT

Es kommt die Nacht
da liebst du

nicht was schön—
was häßlich ist.

Nicht was steigt—
was schon fallen muß.

Nicht wo du helfen kannst—
wo du hilflos bist.

Es ist eine zärtliche Nacht,
die Nacht da du liebst,

was Liebe
nicht retten kann.

TENDER NIGHT

The night comes
when you love

not what is beautiful—
what is ugly.

Not what rises—
what must fall.

Not where you can help—
where you are helpless.

It's a tender night,
the night when you love

what love
cannot save.

ES GIBT DICH

Dein Ort ist
wo Augen dich ansehn
Wo sich die Augen treffen
entstehst du

Von einem Ruf gehalten
immer die gleiche Stimme,
es scheint nur eine zu geben
mit der alle rufen

Du fielest
aber du fällst nicht
Augen fangen dich auf

Es gibt dich
weil Augen dich wollen
dich ansehn und sagen
daß es dich gibt

You Exist

Your place is
where eyes look upon you
Where eyes meet
is where you come into being

Held by a call
always the same voice,
it seems there's only one
with which all call out

You fell
but don't fall
eyes catch you

You are
because eyes desire you
look at you and say
that you exist

Aufbruch ohne Gewicht

Weiße Gardinen, leuchtende Segel
an meinem Fenster
am Hudson,
im zehnten Stock des Hotels
hell in der Sonne gebläht und knatternd im Meerwind.

Versprechen, Ausfahrt
nachhause,
zum Stelldichein mit mir selbst.
Aufbruch ohne Gewicht,
wenn das Herz den Körper verbrannt hat.

Segel so möwenleicht
über das offene Blau.
Das Zimmer ist unterwegs.
Aber das Meer
ist abgesteckt wie ein Acker.

WEIGHTLESS DEPARTURE

White curtains, shining sails
at my window
on the Hudson,
on the tenth floor of the hotel
billowing brightly in the sunlight and rattling in the ocean wind.

Promise, departure
toward home,
for a rendezvous with myself.
Weightless departure
when the heart has burned the body.

Sails as light as gulls
above the open blue.
The room is on the way.
But the sea
is staked out like a tilled field.

FRAGE

Wenn der Vogel ein Fisch wird
dieser kleine Teil von dir
der immer aufstieg

wenn er stumm

in händeloser flügelloser Welt
nicht lernt
Fisch unter Fischen zu sein?

QUESTION

When the bird becomes a fish
this small part of you
that always rose

when it mutely

in a handless wingless world
doesn't learn
to be a fish among fish?

TUNNEL

Dem Andenken Virginia Woolfs

Zu dritt
zu viert
ungezählte, einzeln

allein
gehen wir diesen Tunnel entlang
zur Tag- und Nachtgleiche

drei oder vier von uns
sagen die Worte
dies Wort:

„Fürchte dich nicht"
es blüht
hinter uns her.

TUNNEL

In remembrance of Virginia Woolf

As a threesome
a foursome
uncounted, solitary

we walk along this tunnel
alone
by day or night the same

three or four of us
say the words
this word:

"Fear not"
blooms
behind us as we go.

RÜCKKEHR

Meine Füße wunderten sich
daß neben ihnen Füße gingen
die sich nicht wunderten.

Ich, die ich barfuß gehe
und keine Spur hinterlasse,
immer sah ich den Leuten auf die Schuhe.

Aber die Wege feierten
Wiedersehen
mit meinen schüchternen Füßen.

Am Haus meiner Kindheit blühte
im Februar
der Mandelbaum.

Ich hatte geträumt,
er werde blühen.

RETURN

My feet wondered why
feet walked near them
that didn't wonder.

I, who walk barefoot
and leave no trace,
always looked at people's shoes.

But the paths celebrated
reunion
with my shy feet.

At the house of my childhood
the almond tree bloomed
in February.

I had dreamt
that it would bloom.

BEHÜTET

Ich schlafe im Schutz
meiner Traurigkeit.
Das Leid wie das Glück
baut Mauern.

Ich, ohne Haus,
immer im Schutz dieser Mauer,
wo der Krieg
stillsteht.

Wo ich an der Wunde
von einer Taube
Brustfeder
sterbe.

Sheltered

I sleep under the shelter of
my sorrow.
Sorrow like happiness
builds walls.

I, without a house,
always under the shelter of this wall
where the war
stands still.

Where I, from
the wound of a dove's
breast-feather,
die.

Schneide das Augenlid ab

Schneide das Augenlid ab:
fürchte dich.

Nähe dein Augenlid an:
träume.

Cut Off the Eyelid

Cut off the eyelid:
be afraid.

Sew up your eyelid:
dream.

„Vogel Klage"

Ein Vogel ohne Füße ist die Klage,
kein Ast, keine Hand, kein Nest.

Ein Vogel der sich wundfliegt
im Engen,
ein Vogel der sich verliert
im Weiten,
ein Vogel der ertrinkt
im Meer.
Ein Vogel
der ein Vogel ist,
der ein Stein ist,
der schreit.

Ein stummer Vogel,
den niemand hört.

Bird Lament

Lament is a footless bird,
no branch, no hand, no nest.

A bird that wounds itself flying
in confined spaces,
a bird that loses itself
in the expanse,
a bird that drowns
in the sea.
A bird
that is a bird,
that is a stone
that cries out.

A mute bird
whom no one hears.

WINTERBIENEN

Die Berge zwischen uns,
so sehr viel Luft
zwischen mir und niemand.
Ich bin allein
in sehr viel Luft.
Blaßblumige Wiesen,
Milchstraßen
von Krokus und Primeln,
Frühling.
Die Vögel reisen nach Norden
zu den alten Nestern.
Die Bienen sterben
auf den ersten Blumen,
die Winterbienen.

Ich gehe über die blassen Wiesen ins Tal,
wo die Dörfler einander hassen,
und werfe Briefe ein
für Menschen in Städten.
Ich könnte nicht reisen,
nicht mit den Vögeln,
zu den alten Nestern.
Nicht nach Süden
und nicht nach Norden.
Wenn ich ein Vogel wär,
ich flöge zu niemand.
Ich sehe die blassen Blumen an,
die Blätter vom vorigen Herbst,
und die Winterbienen.

Winter Bees

The mountains between us,
so very much air
between me and no one.
I am alone
in so much air.
Pale-flowering meadow,
Milky Ways
of crocus and primroses,
spring.
The birds fly north
to the old nests.
The bees die
on the first flowers,
the winter bees.

I walk through the pale meadows in the valley
where the villagers hate each another,
and mail letters
to people in cities.
I couldn't travel,
not with the birds
to the old nests.
Not southward
and not northward.
If I were a bird,
I'd fly to no one.
I look at the pale flowers,
the leaves of last fall,
and the winter bees.

SÄMANN

Der große Sämann,
ungerufen,
blies einen Atem von Blumensamen über mich hin
und streute eine Saat
von Kornblumen und rotem Mohn
in meine Weizenfelder.

Das leuchtende Unkraut,
mächtiger Sämann,
wie trenn ich es je
von den Ähren,
ohne die Felder
zu roden?

SOWER

The great sower,
unsummoned,
blew a breath of flower-seeds over me
and scattered a crop
of cornflowers and red poppy
in my wheatfields.

The luminous weed,
powerful sower,
how can I ever separate it
from the blades of grain
without clearing
the fields?

OSTERWIND

Wir haben es den Blumen und Bäumen voraus:
Unsere Jahreszeiten
sind schneller.

Der Tod
steigt im Stengel unseres Traums,
alle Blüten werden dunkel
und fallen.
Kaum ein Herbst. Der Winter kommt
in einer Stunde.

Doch da ist keine Wartezeit,
sicheres Warten
für kahle Zweige.

So wie der Vogel
innehält und sich wendet im Flug,
so jäh, so ohne Grund
dreht sich das Klima des Herzens.
Weiße Flügelsignale im Blau,
Auferstehung
all unserer toten

Blumen
im Osterwind
eines Lächelns.

EASTERWIND

We have this advantage over the flowers and trees:
Our seasons
are faster.

Death
rises up climbs in the stem of our dream,
all the blossoms will darken
and fall.
Barely an autumn. Winter comes
in an hour.

But there is no waiting period,
safe waiting
for the bare branches.

Just as a bird
pauses and turns in flight,
so abruptly and without reason
does the heart's mood turn.
White wing-signals in the blue,
resurrection
of all our dead

flowers
in the Easterwind
of a smile.

SCHÖNER

Schöner sind die Gedichte des Glücks.

Wie die Blüte schöner ist als der Stengel
der sie doch treibt
sind schöner die Gedichte des Glücks.

Wie der Vogel schöner ist als das Ei
wie es schön ist wenn Licht wird
ist schöner das Glück.

Und sind schöner die Gedichte
die ich nicht schreiben werde.

More Beautiful

The poems of happiness are more beautiful.

Just as the blossom is more beautiful than the stem
that propels it
poems of happiness are more beautiful.

Just as the bird is more beautiful than the egg
as it's beautiful when light comes
happiness is more beautiful still.

And more beautiful still are the poems
I will not write.

DEMUT

Demut ist wie ein Brunnen.
Man fällt und fällt
in den bodenlosen Schacht
und aller Trost wird
stetig teurer.

Humility

Humility is like a well.
One falls and falls
into the bottomless shaft
and the cost of all solace
steadily rises.

HERBSTAUGEN

Presse dich eng
an den Boden.

Die Erde
riecht noch nach Sommer,
und der Körper
riecht noch nach Liebe.

Aber das Gras
ist schon gelb über dir.
Der Wind ist kalt
und voll Distelsamen.

Und der Traum, der dir nachstellt,
schattenfüßig,
dein Traum
hat Herbstaugen.

AUTUMN EYES

Press yourself close
to the ground.

The earth
still smells of summer,
and the body
still smells of love.

But the grass
is already yellow above you.
The wind is cold
and full of thistle seeds.

And the dream that still stalks you
shadow-footed,
your dream
has autumn eyes.

BITTE

Wir werden eingetaucht
und mit dem Wasser der Sintflut gewaschen
wir werden durchnäßt
bis auf die Herzhaut

Der Wunsch nach der Landschaft
diesseits der Tränengrenze
taugt nicht
der Wunsch den Blütenfrühling zu halten
der Wunsch verschont zu bleiben
taugt nicht

Es taugt die Bitte
daß bei Sonnenaufgang die Taube
den Zweig vom Ölbaum bringe
Daß die Frucht so bunt wie die Blüte sei
daß noch die Blätter der Rose am Boden
eine leuchtende Krone bilden

Und daß wir aus der Flut
daß wir aus der Löwengrube und dem feurigen Ofen
immer versehrter und immer heiler
stets von neuem
zu uns selbst
entlassen werden

REQUEST

We'll be submerged
and washed with the great flood's waters
we'll be soaked
down to the heart's skin

The desire for the landscape
on this side of tears' border
is of no avail
the desire to halt spring's blossoms
the desire to be spared
is of no avail

What does avail is the request
that the dove bring an olive-branch
at dawn
That the fruit be as colorful as the blossom
that the rose petals on the ground
still be formed into a shining crown

And that from the flood
from the lions' den and from the fiery furnace
we be released
ever more injured and ever more whole
ever anew
to ourselves

BRIEF AUF DEN ANDEREN KONTINENT

Sieh dich nicht um
nach mir

Eurydike
immer mit dir

die Hand
deine Schulter berührend

unter den fernen Bäumen.

LETTER TO THE OTHER CONTINENT

Don't turn around
to face me

Eurydice
always with you

the hand
touching your shoulder

under the distant trees.

DIESER WEITE FLÜGEL

Dieser weite Flügel
mein Wort
mit den unsichtbaren Schwingen
ich bin weitgegangen ich bin gelaufen
mit lidlosen Augen
die Kontinente die Jahre herauf

This Wide Wing

This wide wing
my word
with the invisible pinions
I've gone far I've run
with lidless eyes
up the continents the years

WARNUNG

Wenn die kleinen weißen Straßen
im Süden
die du gegangen bist
sich dir öffnen wie Knospen
voller Sonne
und dich einladen.

Wenn die Welt,
frischgehäutet,
dich aus dem Haus ruft
und dir ein Einhorn
gesattelt
zur Tür schickt.

Dann sollst du hinknieen wie ein Kind
am Fuß deines Betts
und um Bescheidenheit bitten.
Wenn alles dich einlädt,
das ist die Stunde
wo dich alles verläßt.

Warning

When the small white streets
in the south
where you once walked
open themselves to you like buds
full of the sun
and invite you.

When the world,
fresh-skinned,
calls you from your house
and sends a unicorn,
saddled,
to your door.

Then you should kneel down like a child
at the foot of your bed
and pray for humility.
When everything invites you,
that's the hour
when everything deserts you.

Der Baum blüht trotzdem

Der Baum blüht trotzdem
Immer haben die Bäume
auch zur Hinrichtung geblüht

Kirschblüten und
Schmetterlinge
treibt der Wind
auch dem Verurteilten ins
Bett

Sie gehen weiter
Blütenhalter
ohne den Kopf zu wenden
die hellen Reihen

Mancher sagt ein Wort zu dir
oder du glaubst, daß er spricht
im Vorbeigehn

Weil es so still ist

The Tree Blooms Regardless

The tree blooms regardless
Trees have always bloomed
even during an execution

The wind blows
cherry blossoms and
butterflies
even to the condemned
in their bed

They go on
blossom-keepers
without turning their head
the bright rows

Some speak a word to you
or you believe they speak
while passing by

Because it is so still

Noch gestern

Dies Frühjahr ist wie ein Herbst,
ein Abschiednehmen
von allem was kommt.
Das Karussell
fährt vorbei.
Das Karussell mit den großen Tieren.
Nie wieder
wirst du mitfahrn
und warst doch noch gestern
eins von den Kindern die mitfahren müssen.
Du wirst die Geste noch machen,
fast alle machen ja nichts als die Geste,
Leben heißt höflich sein,
kein Spielverderber.
Du ißt das Eis, das man dir in die Hand gibt,
du lächelst, weil alle lächeln,
fast alle machen die Geste der Freude
für die andern.
Gestern hast du gelacht,
weil du gelacht hast.
Du mußt es weiter tun,
du darfst niemand enttäuschen.
Viele Tage werden auch blau sein,
es gibt immer
blaue Tage
wo Lachen leichter ist,
beinah wie früher—
beinah.

Keiner außer dir kennt die kleine Linie,
den Strich auf dem Boden,
den riesigen Strom,
den du nie mehr
überquerst.

JUST YESTERDAY

This spring is like an autumn,
a leave-taking
of all that comes.
The carousel
spins past.
The carousel with the large animals.
Never again
will you ride on it
even though just yesterday
you were one of the children who must ride.
You'll still make the gesture,
almost all of them make nothing but the gesture,
to live means being polite,
not a game-spoiler.
You eat the ice cream cone put in your hand,
you smile because everyone smiles,
almost all make a gesture of joy
for others.
Yesterday you laughed
because you laughed.
You must continue to do so,
you're allowed to disappoint no one.
Many days will also be blue,
there are always
blue days
where laughter is easier,
almost as earlier—
almost.

No one but you knows the thin line,
the stroke on the floor,
the great stream
that you never again
cross over.

WOLKE

Leuchtende Rose
aus Wasser und Sonne
große weiße Wolke
du treibst
ins Dunkle

Wir sind so flüchtig
vor jedem Wind
Das Schneckenhaus bleibt
wir werden aufgelöst
wie du

Unsere Stimmen so hart
und voll Widerstand
wenn der Tag fällt
und du so sanft
auf den Glanz
verzichtest

CLOUD

Shining rose
made of water and sun
great white cloud
you work
in the dark

We are so fleeting
in the face of every wind
The snail's shell remains
we will be dispersed
like you

Our voices so shrill
and full of resistance
when the day ends
and you so softly
renounce
the radiance

GENESIS

Das Wort
der Blick
ändern
erschaffen die Wirklichkeit
den Traum der Wirklichkeit
den Angsttraum der Wirklichkeit
die Wirklichkeit

ihren Kern

Genesis

The word
the view
change
create reality
the dream of reality
the nightmare of reality
reality

their core

Drei Arten Gedichte aufzuschreiben

1
Ein trockenes Flußbett
ein weißes Band von Kieselsteinen
von weitem gesehen
hierauf wünsche ich zu schreiben
in klaren Lettern
oder eine Schutthalde
Geröll
gleitend unter meinen Zeilen
wegrutschend
damit das heikle Leben meiner Worte
ihr Dennoch
ein Dennoch jedes Buchstabens sei

2
Kleine Buchstaben
genaue
damit die Worte leise kommen
damit die Worte sich einschleichen
damit man hingehen muß
zu den Worten
sie suchen in dem weißen
Papier
leise
man merkt nicht wie sie eintreten
durch die Poren
Schweiß der nach innen rinnt

Angst
meine
unsere
und das Dennoch jedes Buchstabens

Three Ways to Write Poems Down

1
A dry riverbed
a white band of pebbles
seen from a distance
I want to write on them
in clear letters
or a pile of rubble
scree
sliding under my lines
slipping away
so that the tenuous life of my words
their nevertheless
might be a nevertheless of each letter

2
Small letters
exact
so that the words come quietly
so that the words creep in
so that one must go
to the words
search for them in the white
paper
quietly
one doesn't notice how they enter
through the pores
sweat that trickles inwardly

Fear
my
our
and the nevertheless of each letter

3
Ich will einen Streifen Papier
so groß wie ich
ein Meter sechzig
darauf ein Gedicht
das schreit
sowie einer vorübergeht
schreit in schwarzen Buchstaben
das etwas Unmögliches verlangt
Zivilcourage zum Beispiel
diesen Mut den kein Tier hat
Mit-Schmerz zum Beispiel
Solidarität statt Herde
Fremd-Worte
heimisch zu machen im Tun

Mensch
Tier das Zivilcourage hat
Mensch
Tier das den Mit-Schmerz kennt
Mensch Fremdwort-Tier Wort-Tier
Tier
das Gedichte schreibt
Gedicht
das Unmögliches verlangt
von jedem der vorbeigeht
dringend
unabweisbar
als rufe es
„Trink Coca-Cola"

3
I want a scrap of paper
as large as I am
one meter sixty
and on it a poem
that cries out
the moment someone passes by
cries out in black letters
that demand something impossible
like the courage of one's convictions for example
like the courage no animal has
shared pain for example
solidarity instead of the herd
to make foreign-words
our own in what is done

human being
animal with the courage of its own convictions
human being
animal who knows shared pain
human being foreign-word-animal word-animal
animal
who writes poems
poem
that demands the impossible
of each one who passes by
urgently
irrefutably
as if calling out
"Drink Coca Cola"

Salva Nos

1
Heute rufen wir
heute nennen wir.
Eine Stimme
die ein Wort sagt
das Widerfahrene

mit etwas Luft die in uns aufsteigt
mit nichts als unserm Atem
Vokale und Konsonanten
zu einem Worte fügend
einem Namen
es zähmt
das Unzähmbare
es zwingt
einen Herzschlag lang
unser Ding zu sein.

2
Dies ist unsere Freiheit
die richtigen Namen nennend
furchtlos
mit der kleinen Stimme

einander rufend
mit der kleinen Stimme
das Verschlingende beim Namen nennen
mit nichts als unserm Atem

salva nos ex ore leonis
den Rachen offen halten
in dem zu wohnen
nicht unsere Wahl ist.

Save Us

1
Today we call out
today we name.
A voice
that speaks a word
that which you've experienced

with a bit of air that rises up in us
with nothing other than our breath
vowels and consonants
melding into a word
a name
it tames
the untamable
it demands
for one heartbeat
to be our thing.

2
This is our freedom
naming the right names
fearlessly
with the small voice

calling each other
with the small voice
to call what devours by name
with nothing but our breath

salva nos ex ore leonis[6]
to hold open the mouth
in which we do not choose
to dwell.

ALTERNATIVE

Ich lebte auf einer Wolke
einem fliegenden Teller
und las keine Zeitung.

Meine zärtlichen Füße
gingen die Wege nicht mehr
die sie nicht gehen konnten.

Einander tröstend
wie zwei Tauben
wurden sie jeden Tag kleiner.

Gewiß ich war unnütz.

Der Wolkenteller zerbrach
ich fiel in die Welt
eine Welt aus Schmirgelpapier.

Die Handflächen tun mir weh
die Füße hassen einander.
Ich weine.

Und bin unnütz.

ALTERNATIVE

I lived on a cloud
on a flying plate
and read no newspaper.

My tender feet
no longer walked the paths
they could not tread.

Consoling each other
like two doves
they became smaller each day.

Certainly I was useless.

The cloud-plate broke apart
I fell into the world
a world made of sandpaper.

The palms of my hand hurt
my feet hate each other.
I weep.

And am useless.

TOPOGRAFIE

Ich bin eine bunte
Topographie.

Blaue und rote Fahnen
auf weißem Grund
markieren die Hügel
wo aller Widerstand

der rebellischen Heere
deinem Durchbruch erlag

und meine Soldaten
zum Feind desertierten.

Topography

I am a colorful
topography.

Blue and red flags
on a white background
mark the hills
where the resistance

of the rebellious armies
fell victim to your breakthrough

and my soldiers
deserted to the enemy.

ALLE MEINE SCHIFFE

Alle meine Schiffe
haben die Häfen vergessen
und meine Füße den Weg.
Es wird nicht gesät und nicht geerntet
denn es ist keine Vergangenheit
und keine Zukunft,
kaum eine Bühne im Tag.
Nur der kleine
zärtliche Abstand
zwischen dir und mir,
den du nicht verminderst.

ALL MY SHIPS

All my ships
have forgotten the harbors
and my feet the way.
There won't be planting and harvesting
because there's no past
and no future,
hardly a stage during the day.
Only a small
tender gap
between you and me,
which you don't diminish.

GEGENGEWICHT

Wie kann ich
in meinem blauesten Kleid
und riefe ich alle die blühenden Zweige
und alle Nachtigallen zu Hilfe

wie kann ich mit Lachen oder mit Tränen
das Gleichgewicht halten
der anderen Schale
in der die Welt liegt

eine Nuß aus Blei?

COUNTERWEIGHT

How can I
in my bluest dress
even if I were to call all the blooming branches
and all the nightingales for help

how can I with laughter or with tears
maintain the balance
with the other bowl
in which the world lies

a nut made of lead?

WINDGESCHENKE

Die Luft ein Archipel
von Duftinseln.
Schwaden von Lindenblüten
und sonnigem Heu,
süß vertraut,
stehen und warten auf mich
als umhüllten mich Tücher,
von lange her
aus sanftem Zuhaus
von der Mutter gewoben.

Ich bin wie im Traum
und kann den Windgeschenken
kaum glauben.
Wolken von Zärtlichkeit
fangen mich ein,
und das Glück beißt
seinen kleinen Zahn
in mein Herz.

The Wind's Gifts

The air an archipelago
of fragrant islands.
Clouds of lime-tree blossoms
and sunny hay,
sweetly familiar,
stand still and wait for me
as though shawls wrapped me,
in times past,
woven by the mother
of a tender home.

I am as in a dream
and can scarcely believe
the wind's gifts.
Clouds of tenderness
capture me,
and happiness bites
its small tooth
in my heart.

TALFAHRT

Die ewigen Hirten
trotz der Intensivhaltung der Tiere
die ewigen Weiden
das goldene Sterben der Bäume

Ihr mechanisiertes
Sterben
der Tiermaschinen

Unser
mechanisiertes
Leben

Du streichst mit der Hand
von ferne
über die grüne Haut eines Bergs

Decline[7]

The eternal shepherds
in spite of the factory-farming of animals
the eternal meadows
the golden dying of the trees

Their mechanized
death
of the animal-machines

Our
mechanized
life

With your hand
you stroke the mountain's green skin
from afar

NACHT

Man hat mich Tote aufs Wasser gelegt
ich fahre die Flüsse hinunter

die Rhône den Rhein den Guadalquivir
den Haifischfluß in den Tropen.

Am Meer die Särge.
Ich ohne Münze zwischen den Zähnen

ich treibe in meinem Bett
an den barmherzigen

Bewahrern
geliebter Toter vorbei

überzählig
unnützer als Treibholz

in den Tag.

NIGHT

I have been laid a dead one upon the waters
I make my way down the rivers

the Rhone the Rhine the Guadalquivir
the Shark River in the tropics.

By the sea the coffins.
I without a coin between my teeth

I drift in my bed
past the compassionate

protectors
of the beloved dead

superfluous
more useless than driftwood

into the day.

WINTER

Die Vögel, schwarze Früchte
in den kahlen Ästen.
Die Bäume spielen Verstecken mit mir,
ich gehe wie unter Leuten
die ihre Gedanken verbergen
und bitte die dunklen Zweige
um ihre Namen.

Ich glaube, daß sie blühen werden
—innen ist grün—
daß du mich liebst
und es verschweigst.

WINTER

The birds, black fruit
in the bare branches.
The trees play hide-and-seek with me.
I wander as among people
who hide their thoughts
and ask the dark boughs
their names.

I believe that they'll blossom
—the inside is green—
that you love me
and conceal it.

WUNSCH

Ich möchte von den Dingen die ich sehe
wie von dem Blitz
gespalten werden
Ich will nicht daß sie vorüberziehen
farblos bunte
sie schwimmen auf meiner Netzhaut
sie treiben vorbei
in die dunkle Stelle
am Ende der Erinnerung

WISH

I'd like to be split open
by the things I see
as from a lightning bolt
I don't want them to pass by
pale colorful
they swim on my retina
they float by
into the dark place
at the end of memory

WEIHNACHTSBOTSCHAFT

Die Heiliggeistkirche hell erleuchtet…
Das Johannesevangelium.
Am Anfang war das Wort.
Dann das Lukasevangelium.

Und der Engel mit dem Schwert gab in
dieser Nacht die Paradiespforte wieder frei.

„Die Tür zum Paradies" hieß es.
Ich hatte es mir nie überlegt,
dass es ja weiter bewacht und verboten ist.

Das war für mich die Weihnachtsbotschaft:
dass in dieser Nacht
der Cherub den Wachposten räumte.

CHRISTMAS TIDINGS

The Church of the Holy Spirit brightly lit…
The Gospel of John.
In the beginning was the Word.
Then the Gospel of Luke.

And the angel with the sword on this night
opened the Gate of Paradise again.

"The door to paradise" it was named.
I had never considered
that it was guarded and forbidden.

That for me was the good news of Christmas:
that on this night
the cherub dispersed the guardsman.

ABZÄHLEN DER REGENTROPFENSCHNUR

Ich zähle die Regentropfen an den Zweigen,
sie glänzen, aber sie fallen nicht,
schimmernde Schnüre von Tropfen
an den kahlen Zweigen.
Die Wiese sieht mich an
mit großen Augen aus Wasser.
Die goldgrünen Weidenkätzchen
haben ein triefendes Fell.
Keine Biene besucht sie.
Ich will sie einladen
sich an meinem Ofen zu trocken.

Ich sitze auf einem Berg
und habe alles,
das Dach und die Wände,
das Bett und den Tisch,
den heißen Regen im Badezimmer
und den Ofen mit löwenfarbener Mähne,
der atmet wie ein Tier
oder ein Mitmensch.
Und die Postfrau
die den Brief bringen würde
auf meinen Berg.

Aber die Weidenkätzchen
treten nicht ein
und der Brief kommt nicht,
denn die Regentropfen
wollen sich nicht zählen lassen.

COUNTING THE RAINDROP CORD

I count the raindrops on the branches,
they gleam but don't fall,
shimmering cords of drops
on the bare branches.
The meadow looks me over
with large eyes of water.
The gold-green pussy willows
have a dripping fur.
No bees come to visit them.
I want to invite them
to dry themselves off on my stove.

I sit on a mountain
and have everything,
roof and walls,
bed and table,
the hot rain in the bathroom
and the stove with a lion-colored mane
that breathes like an animal
or a fellow human being.
And the mail carrier
who would bring the mail
to my mountain.

But the pussy willows
don't come in
and the letter doesn't arrive
because the raindrops
don't want to let themselves be counted.

WARTE AUF NICHTS

Vom Baum des Himmels
sind die Wolken auf die Erde gefallen.
Das Land ist gefleckt
von großen dunklen Blättern.

In den Straßen der Traurigen
werden die Fensterrahmen
in der Farbe des Himmels gemalt,
in der Farbe der Sonne
in den lichtlosen Häusern.

Taubenschläge auf den Dächern
für ein hellgefiedertes Gestern,
das nicht wiederkehrt.

Nur das Geläute am Waldrand.
Wellen von kleinen Glocken
bis in das Zimmer.
Zieh die Schuhe aus,
netze die Füße.

Warte auf nichts
als das Läuten
der kleinen Glocken
am Waldrand.

WAIT FOR NOTHING

The clouds have fallen to the earth
from the tree of heaven.
The land is speckled
with large dark leaves.

In the streets of those who are sad
the window frames are being painted
in the color of the sky,
in the color of the sun
in the lightless houses.

Pigeon lofts on the roofs
for a brightly-feathered yesterday
that does not return.

Only the ringing at woods' edge.
Waves of little bells
all the way to the room.
Take the shoes off,
bind the feet.

Wait for nothing
other than the peal
of the little bells
at woods' edge.

ZUR INTERPUNKTION

Weil sich die Neger
fürchten
weil sich die Weißen
fürchten
fürchten meine Worte
ein einfaches Komma
eingesperrt zwischen Satzzeichen
offene Fenster
offene Zeilen
meine Worte haben Angst
vor dem Verrat
des Menschen
an dem Menschen
versuche
ihn nicht
lasse alle Türen
offen
presse uns nicht
uns Wolken

On Punctuation

Because blacks
fear
because whites
fear
my words fear
a simple comma
trapped between punctuation marks
open windows
open lines
my words are afraid
of the betrayal
by one person
of another
don't
tempt him
leave all the doors
open
don't press us
us clouds

IRGENDWANN

Irgendwann
eine eiternde Wunde
ein Schrei
nicht hörbar
wird es aufbrechen
mit einer Kinderstirn wird es einhergehn
barfüßig
waffenlos
dieses Leuchten
Jahrhunderte
Gesellschaftsordnungen
können ihm nichts tun.

Es wird sein von immer zu immer
wie die Tränen gleich sind auf allen Gesichtern
durch die Kontinente, die Jahrhunderte,
wenn es kommt
dieses Lächeln
gleich hell auf den Gesichtern
aller Hautfarben
dieses Einverständnis
ist und wird gleich sein
immer
das Lächeln
der Verzicht.

Sometime

Sometime
a festering wound
a scream
inaudible
it will break open
it will move about with a child's brow
barefoot
weaponless
this glow
centuries
societal rules
can't do a thing to it.

It will be from always to always
just as tears are the same on all faces
across the continents, the centuries,
when it arrives
this smile
equally bright on all the faces
of every skin color
this consent
is and will be the same
always
the smile
the renunciation.

ENTFERNUNG

Die Entfernung
eines Kranken

von dem der bei ihm sitzt
ist nicht weiter

als die Kontinente
voneinander.

Unendlich weit.
Nur dieses

Hand in Hand.
Und doch es gilt nur

unter Gehenden.

DISTANCE

The distance
of a sick person

from the one who sits beside him
is not farther

than the continents
from each other.

Endlessly distant.
Only this

hand in hand.
And yet this is valid only

among the departing.

GEGENWART

Wer auf der Schwelle seines Hauses geweint hat
wie nicht je ein fremder Bettler.
Wer die Nacht auf den Dielen
neben dem eigenen Lager verbrachte.
Wer die Toten bat
sich wegzuwenden von seiner Scham.

Dessen Sohle betritt die Straße nicht wieder,
sein Gestern und Morgen
sind durch ein Jahrhundert getrennt
und reichen sich nie mehr die Hand.
Die Rose verblüht ihm nicht.
Der Pfeil trifft ihn nie.

Doch fast erschreckt ihn der Trost
wenn sich ein sichtbarer Flügel wölbt,
sein zitterndes Licht
zu beschützen.

PRESENT

Whoever has wept on the threshold of his house
as a foreign beggar might.
Whoever has spent the night on floorboards
next to his own bed.
Whoever has bidden the dead
to turn away from his shame.

That one's soles no longer tread the street,
his yesterday and tomorrow
are separated by a century
and no longer reach out to each other.
The rose does not fade for him.
The arrow never strikes him.

But solace almost scares him
when a visible wing bends over
to protect
his trembling light.

Das goldene Seil

Nichts ist so flüchtig
wie die Begegnung.

Wir spielen wie die Kinder,
wir laden uns ein und aus
als hätten wir ewig Zeit.
Wir scherzen mit dem Abschied,
wir sammeln noch Tränen wie Klicker
und versuchen ob die Messer schneiden.
Da wird schon der Name
gerufen.
Da ist schon die Pause
vorbei.

Wir halten
uns bange fest
an dem goldenen Seil
und widerstreben dem Aufbruch.
Aber es reißt.
Wir treiben hinaus:
hinweg aus der gleichen Stadt,
hinweg aus der gleichen Welt,
unter die gleiche,
die alles vermengende
Erde.

The Golden Cord

Nothing is as fleeting
as an encounter.

We play like children,
we invite and disinvite ourselves
as if we had endless time.
We joke around with the departure,
we still collect tears like marbles
and test to see if knives cut.
Already the name is being
called.
Already the break is
over.

We keep
a fearful grip
on the golden cord
and struggle against the departure.
But it breaks.
We drift away:
away from the same city,
away from the same world,
beneath the same earth
that mixes everything
together.

WAHL

Ein Mandelbaum sein
eine kleine Wolke
in Kopfhöhe über dem Boden
ganz hell
einmal im Jahr

Einer im kleinen Stoßtrupp
des Frühlings
keinem zu Leid als sich selber
im Glauben an einen blauen Tag
vor Kälte verbrennen

Ein kleiner Mandelbaum sein
am Südhang der Pyrenäen
oder im Rheintal
der bleibt und wächst
wo er gepflanzt ist

Aber entlang gehen
bei diesem Mandelbaum
oder ihn plötzlich sehn
wenn der Zug
aus dem Tunnel kommt

Lachen und Weinen und die unmögliche
Wahl haben
und nichts ganz recht tun
und nichts ganz verkehrt
und vielleicht alles verlieren

Choice

To be an almond tree
a small cloud
at head-height above the ground
completely bright
once each year

One of the assault squads
of spring
troubling no one but themselves
believing in a blue day
burning from the cold

To be a small almond tree
on the south face of the Pyrenees
or in the Rhine valley
one that stays and grows
where it was planted

But to pass along
beside this almond tree
or to see it suddenly
when the train
comes out of the tunnel

Laughing and crying and having the impossible
choice
and doing nothing entirely right
and nothing entirely wrong
and perhaps losing everything

Doch mit Ja und Nein und Für-immer-vorbei
nicht müde werden
sondern dem Wunder
leise
wie einem Vogel,
die Hand hinhalten

Yet not to grow weary
of Yes and No and Forever-Gone
but to hold the hand out
quietly
to the miracle,
as if to a bird

TREULOSE KAHNFAHRT

Aber der Traum ist ein Kahn
zu dem falschen Ufer.
Du steigst ein
an dem schimmernden Holzsteg des Gestern.
Du bist eingeladen
zu einer Fahrt über rosa Wolken
unter rosa Wolken,
wolkengleich.

Ein Hauch der Luft
du bist so leicht,
der Kahn so steuerlos,
das Wasser so spiegelglatt.
So sanft verlierst du die Richtung:
du bist noch unterwegs nach der Wiese im Licht,
wenn der Sand schon unter dem Kiel knirscht
im Schatten der Weiden.

Unfaithful Boat Ride

But the dream is a boat
to the wrong shore.
You get in
at the shimmering wooden dock of yesterday.
You're invited
to take a ride over the pink clouds
under the pink clouds,
cloudlike.

A wisp of air
you're that light,
the boat so rudderless,
the water smooth as a mirror.
Ever so softly you lose your bearings:
you're still on your way to the meadow in light
as the sand scrunches under the keel
in the willows' shadow.

AUF DER ANDERN SEITE DES MONDS

Auf der anderen Seite des Monds
gehen
in goldene Kleider gehüllt
deine wirklichen Tage
sie wohnen
wie sonst du
in Helle
verscheucht von hier
weggescheucht
wandeln sie dort
du weißt es sind deine.

Du aber empfängst
Morgen nach Morgen
ihre Stellvertreter:
fremder
als jedes fremde Land.
Du weißt
die deinen
wandeln in Helle
sie ziehen Tag um Tag
neben dir her
nur auf der anderen Seite des Monds.

On the Other Side of the Moon

On the other side of the moon
your real days
pass
wrapped in golden clothing
they live
as you normally do
in brightness
driven away from here
scared off
they walk about there
you know they're yours

But morning after morning
you receive
their deputy:
more foreign
than any foreign country.
You know
your own
walk about in brightness
day after day they draw
near to you
only on the other side of the moon.

Die Botschafter

Die Botschafter
kommen von weither
von jenseits der Mauer

barfuß
kommen sie
den weiten Weg

um dies Wort abzugeben.
Einer steht vor dir
in fernen Kleidern

er bringt das Wort Ich
er breitet die Arme aus
er sagt das Wort Ich

mit diesem trennenden Wort
eben saht ihr euch an
ist er nicht mehr

geht in dir weiter.

THE AMBASSADORS

The ambassadors
come from a distance
from the other side of the wall

barefoot
they come
from far away

to hand over this word.
One of them stands before you
in clothes from distant places

he brings the word I
he opens his arms wide
he says the word I

with this distinguishing word
you just looked at each other
he no longer is

goes on in you.

IN VOLLER FAHRT

Wir sitzen in einem Zug
niemand fragt ob wir
aussteigen wollen
und fahren auf eine Brücke zu
und die Brücke wird brechen
Diese Brücke oder die nächste
wird brechen

Wie weh du mir tust
wie weh ich dir tu
wo wir dahinfahr'n
in solcher Eile
auf eine Brücke zu—
die nicht tragen wird

At Full Speed

Shining soft
We're sitting in a train
no one asks if we
want to get out
and travel toward a bridge
and the bridge will crumble
This bridge or the next
will crumble

How much you hurt me
How much I hurt you
as we ride on
in such haste
toward a bridge—
that won't support us

WIR NEHMEN ABSCHIED

Wir nehmen Abschied
freiwillig.
Was wir lieben bleibt
puppengroß
auf einem Streifen Zement
als könnten wir
die Puppe
so wiederfinden.

Wir behalten das
Heimweh nach dem Abschied
lange
nach der Rückkehr.

We Take Leave

We take leave
voluntarily.
What we love remains
doll-sized
on a strip of cement
as if we could
find the doll
this way again.

We retain the
yearning for home after leaving
long
after the return.

ÄNDERUNGEN

Neben meinem Kopf
ich lege ein Stück Weißbrot neben meinen Kopf
mit seinen goldenen Rändern
gieße Wein dazu
streue Salz
aus meinem Kissen wächst eine Laube
mein Bettuch wird zum Tischtuch
das Tischtuch
zum Leichentuch

CHANGES

Next to my head
I lay a piece of white bread next to my head
with its golden edges
and then pour wine
sprinkle salt
an arbor grows out of my pillow
my bedsheet becomes a tablecloth
and the tablecloth
a burial shroud

Geborgenheit

Morgens in der weißen
Geborgenheit einer Badewanne
ohne Wasser
denke ich an den Baumstamm
in dem ich liegen möchte,
glatt, hell, kantenlos,
als sei ich in ihm zuhause
wie eine Dryade.
Niemand wird mich in
einem Baumstamm
oder in der Wanne
begraben wollen,
auf einem Friedhof
den ich wähle,
weil ihn die Abendsonne trifft,
aber zu dessen Sprengel
ich, die Weggezogene,
die nirgends Eingetragene,
in keiner Kirche, in keiner Stadt,
der die Briefe von Land zu Land
nachgeschickt werden,
nicht
gehöre.

SECURITY

Each morning in the white
safety of a bathtub
without water
I think of the tree trunk
in which I'd like to lie,
smooth, bright, edgeless,
as if I were at home in it
like a nymph.
No one will want to
bury me
in a tree trunk
or in a tub,
in a cemetery
that I choose
because the evening sun falls upon it,
but to whose parish
I, the one who moved away,
who is nowhere registered,
in no church, in no city,
to whom letters had to be forwarded
from country to country,
do not
belong.

ARS LONGA

Der Atem
in einer Vogelkehle
der Atem der Luft
in den Zweigen.

Das Wort
wie der Wind selbst
sein heiliger Atem
geht es aus und ein.

Immer findet der Atem
Zweige
Wolken
Vogelkehlen.

Immer das Wort
das heilige Wort
einen Mund.

Art Is Long[8]

The breath
in a bird's throat
the breath of the air
in the branches.

The word
like the wind itself
its holy breath
goes out and in.

The breath always finds
branches
clouds
bird's throats.

Always finds the word
the holy word
a mouth.

Ich bewahre mich nicht

Ich fiel mir aus der Hand
Ich flügelschlagend
fiel auf den Kies
die Flügel schlagend

Mit ausgebreiteten Flügeln
ich bewahre mich nicht
mit ausgebreiteten Flügeln
verlaß ich's

I Don't Protect Myself

I fell from my hand
I wing-beating
fell on the gravel
beating my wings

With outstretched wings
I don't protect myself
with outstretched wings
I abandon it

DIE HEILIGEN

Die Heiligen in den Kapellen
wollen begraben werden, ganz nackt,
in Särgen aus Kistenholz
und wo niemand sie findet:
in einem Weizenfeld
oder bei einem Apfelbaum
dem sie blühen helfen
als ein Krumen Erde.
Die reichen Gewänder, das Gold und die Perlen,
alle Geschenke der fordernden Geber,
lassen sie in den Sakristeien,
das Los, das verlieren wird, unter dem Sockel.
Sie wollen ihre Schädel und Finger einsammeln
und aus den Glaskästen nehmen
und sie von den Papierrosen ohne Herbst
und den gefaßten Steinen
zu den welken Blumenblättern bringen
und zu den Kieseln am Fluß.

Sie verstehen zu leiden,
das haben sie bewiesen.
Sie haben für einen Augenblick
ihr eigenes Schwergewicht überwunden.
Das Leid trieb sie hoch,
als ihr Herz den Körper verzehrte.
Sie stiegen wie Ballons, federleicht,
und lagen in der Schwebe auf ihrem wehen Atem
als sei er eine Pritsche.
Deshalb lächeln sie jetzt,
wenn sie an Feiertagen
auf schweren geschmückten Podesten
auf den Schultern von achtzig Gläubigen
(denen man das Brot zur Stärkung voranträgt)
in Baumhöhe durch die Straßen ziehn.

The Saints

The saints in the chapel
want to be buried, utterly naked,
in coffins made from wooden crates
and in a place where no one can find them:
in a wheatfield
or near an apple tree
which they can help to bloom
as a crumb of topsoil.
The rich vestments, the gold and the pearls,
all these gifts from overbearing donors,
they leave in the sacristies,
and under the pedestal, the lottery ticket that will lose.
They want to gather up their skulls and fingers,
and take them out of the glass cases
and bring them from the unfading paper roses
and inlaid gemstones
to wilted flower petals
and to the river's pebbles.

They know how to suffer,
they've shown it.
They've overcome for a moment
their own heaviness.
Suffering exalted them
as their hearts consumed their bodies.
They rose up like balloons, feather-light,
and lay hovering on their aching breath
as if it were a hard bed.
That's why they're smiling now
when on feast-days they're pulled
atop heavy decorated pedestals
on the shoulders of eighty believers
(with bread for their refreshment carried on ahead)
at tree-height through the streets.

Doch sie sind müde
auf den Podesten zu stehn
und uns anzuhören.
Sie sind wund vom Willen zu helfen,
wund, Rammbock vor dem Beter zu sein,
der erschrickt
wenn das Gebet ihm gewährt wird,
weil Annehmen
so viel schwerer ist als Bitten
und weil jeder die Gabe nur sieht
die auf dem erwarteten Teller gereicht wird.
Weil jeder doch immer von Neuem
in den eigenen Schatten tritt,
der ihn schmerzt.
Sie sehen den unsichtbaren Kreis
um den Ziehbrunnen,
in dem wir uns drehn
wie in einem Gefängnis.
Jeder will den Quell
in dem eigenen Grundstück,
keiner mag in den Wald gehen.
Der Bruder wird nie
das Feuer wie Abel richten
und doch immer gekränkt sein.

Sie sehen uns wieder und wieder
aneinander vorbeigehn
die Minute versäumend.
Wir halten die Augen gesenkt.
Wir hören den Ruf,
aber wir heben sie nicht.
Erst danach.
Es macht müde zu sehn
wie wir uns umdrehn
und weinen.
Immer wieder

But they're weary
of standing on these pedestals
and listening to us.
They're raw from the will to help,
raw of being battering rams in front of one who prays,
who is shocked
when his prayer is granted,
because accepting
is so much more difficult than asking
and because each one only sees the gift
that is handed over on the expected plate.
Because each one treads ever anew
in their own shadow,
which hurts them.
They see the invisible circle
around the wells
in which we turn ourselves
as in a prison.
Each wants the spring's source
on their own property,
and no one wants to go into the forest.
The brother never wants to prepare
the fire as Abel did
and remain forever troubled.

They see us over and over again
walking past each other,
wasting time.
We lower our eyes.
We hear the call,
but don't raise them.
Only afterwards.
It's tiring to see
how we turn
and weep.
Again and again

uns umdrehn und weinen.
Und die Bitten zu hören
um das gestern Gewährte.
Nachts wenn wir nicht schlafen können
in den Betten, in die wir uns legen.
Sie sind müde
Vikare des Unmöglichen auf Erden
zu sein, des gestern Möglichen.
Sie möchten Brennholz
in einem Herdfeuer sein
und die Milch der Kinder wärmen
wie der silberne Stamm einer Ulme.

Sie sind müde, aber sie bleiben,
der Kinder wegen.
Sie behalten den goldenen Reif auf dem Kopf,
den goldenen Reif,
der wichtiger ist als die Milch.
Denn wir essen Brot,
aber wir leben von Glanz.
Wenn die Lichter angehn
vor dem Gold,
zerlaufen die Herzen der Kinder
und beginnen zu leuchten
vor den Altären.
Und darum gehen sie nicht:
damit es eine Tür gibt,
eine schwere Tür
für Kinderhände,
hinter der das Wunder
angefaßt werden kann.

turning and weeping.
And hearing the pleas
for what was yesterday granted.
Nights when we can't sleep
in the beds in which we lie.
They're weary
of being vicars of the impossible on earth,
of what yesterday was possible.
They want to be firewood
in a hearth-fire,
and warm the children's milk
like the silver trunk of an elm.

They're weary, but they abide
for the children's sake.
They keep the golden halo on their head,
the golden halo
that is more important than milk.
For we eat bread,
but we live from radiance.
When the lights begin to shine
before the gold,
the children's hearts are overcome
and begin to shine
before the altars.
And that's why they don't leave:
so that there will be a door,
a heavy door
for children's hands
behind which the miracle
can be touched.

ÄLTER WERDEN

Antwort an Christa Wolf

> „Du weinst um das Nachlassen…und, so unglaublich es
> sein mag, den unvermeidlichen Verfall der Sehnsucht."
> („Kindheitsmuster")

1
Die Sehnsucht
nach Gerechtigkeit
nimmt nicht ab
Aber die Hoffnung

Die Sehnsucht
nach Frieden
nicht
Aber die Hoffnung

Die Sehnsucht nach Sonne
nicht
täglich kann das Licht kommen
durchkommen

Das Licht ist immer da
eine Flugzeugfahrt reicht
zur Gewißheit
Aber die Liebe

der Tode und Auferstehungen fähig

wie wir selbst
und wie wir

der Schonung bedürftig

GROWING OLDER

An answer to Christa Wolf

> *"You weep over diminishment…and, however unbelievable*
> *this might be, over the unavoidable decline of yearning."*
> (Patterns of Childhood)[9]

1
The yearning
for justice
does not decrease
But the hope

The yearning
for freedom
does not
But the hope

The yearning for sun
does not
daily the light can come
come through

The light is always there
a plane flight suffices
to confirm this
But the love

capable of death and resurrections

like we ourselves
and like we

needing care

2

Gegen die Angst vor dem Mitmensch
„Der Mensch ist dem Menschen ein Gott"
das Veronal in der Tasche

3

Hand in Hand mit der Sprache
bis zuletzt

2
Against the fear toward a fellow human being
"The person is, for another person, a god"
the barbiturate in the pocket

3
Hand in hand with language
to the last

UNSERE LANGEN SCHATTEN

Unsere langen Schatten
im Sternenlicht
und der Wein auf der Erde
Wie eng am Tode
führt unser Weg
Oh Lieber bedenk es
wie geliehen wir sind
wie flüchtig das Unsre
das Gefühl und wir selbst
Was Du heute an Ich sparst
und nicht bis zum Rand gibst
ist morgen vielleicht
so traurig und unnütz
wie die Puppe
nach dem Begräbnis des
Kinds

Nur die klingende
bis zur äußersten
Haut des Herzens gespannte
Stunde besteht

Our Long Shadows

Our long shadows
in starlight
and wine upon the earth
How close to death
our way leads
Oh my darling consider
how borrowed we are
how fleeting what is ours
the feeling and we ourselves
What you hold back of the I today
and don't give to the fullest
may tomorrow be
as sad and useless
as the doll
after the child's
burial

Only the ringing hour
stretched all the way
to the outermost layer
of the heart endures

FÜNF AUSREISELIEDER

1
HIER

Ungewünschte Kinder
meine Worte
frieren.

Kommt
ich will euch
auf meine warmen
Fingerspitzen
setzen
Schmetterlinge im Winter.

Die Sonne
blaß wie ein Mond
scheint auch hier
in diesem Land
wo wir das Fremdsein
zu Ende kosten.

2
AUSREISEGEDICHT

Die Gegenstände sehen mich kommen
barfuß
ich gebe ihnen die Freiheit wieder
meinem Bett das mein Bett sein wollte
meinem Tisch
den Wänden die auf mich zu warten versprachen
wie die Wände der Kindheit.
Meine sanften Gegenstände
ihr wolltet mich sammeln.

Five Songs for Leaving the Country

1
Here

Unwanted children
my words
freeze.

Come
I want to
set you
on my warm
fingertips
butterflies in winter.

The sun
pale as a moon
shines even here
in this land
where we taste
being foreign fully.

2
Departure Poem

The objects see me coming
barefoot
I give them freedom again
I give my bed that wanted to be my bed
my table
and the walls that promised to wait for me
like the walls of childhood.
My soft objects
they wanted to gather me.

Gegenstände
ihr seht mich gehn.

3

ICH FLÜCHTE MICH ZU DEM KLEINSTEN DING

Ich flüchte mich zu dem kleinsten Ding
der Ewigkeit eines Mooses
feucht
fingergroß
von der Kindheit
bis heute.

Ich Gulliver
lege mein Gesicht in dies Moos
Gulliver
dessen Schritt
stehe ich auf
die Grenze des Lands überschreitet.

4

KEINE ZEIT FÜR ABENTEUER

Wenn die Enden der Welt dir Vorstädte sind

du kennst den Geruch
du rückst die Buchstaben nebeneinander
die öffnen
und gehst hinein
nicht
in Weite
in andere Enge.

Objects
you see me go.

3
I Flee to the Smallest Thing

I flee to the smallest thing
to the eternity of a moss
moist
finger-sized
from childhood
until today.

I Gulliver
lay my face in this moss
Gulliver
whose step
I stand up
crosses over the land's boundary.

4
No Time for Adventure

When the ends of the world are suburbs for you

you know the smell
you place the letters next to each another
which open
and you enter in
not
into vastness
into a different narrowing.

Aus deiner Tür
wohin denn?
Wohnst du nicht häuslich
wie jeder
einsam
wie jeder
im Schlund deines Tigers?

Nein, es ist keine Zeit
für Abenteuer.

5
„SILENCE AND EXILE"

Unverlierbares Exil
du trägst es bei dir
du schlüpfst hinein
gefaltetes Labyrinth
Wüste
einsteckbar.

From your door
whither then?
Don't you make yourself at home
like everyone
lonely
like everyone
in the jaws of your tiger?

No, it's no time
for adventure.

5
"Silence and Exile"

Unlosable exile
you carry it with you
you slip inside
folded labyrinth
wilderness
portable.

ORIENTIERUNG

Für Minne

Mein Herz, diese Sonnenblume
auf der Suche
nach dem Licht.

Welchem
der lang vergangenen Schimmer
hebst du den Kopf zu
an den dunklen Tagen?

ORIENTATION

For Minne

My heart, this sunflower
in search
of light.

To which
of the long-gone glimmerings
do you raise your head
on the dark days?

FALLSCHIRM

Tränennasses Gedicht
der äußersten Einsamkeit
du Netz über dem Abgrund
weißer Fallschirm
der sich öffnet im Sturz

Ein Engel hätte Flügel
unter einem Engel
weicht der Boden nicht
Ein Engel erhält nie
verwirrende Botschaft
über sich selbst

PARACHUTE

Tear-soaked poem
of the utmost loneliness
you net above the abyss
white parachute
that opens in a fall

An angel would have wings
beneath an angel
the earth does not give way
An angel would never receive
a confusing message
about itself

ANTWORT

Für E. W. P.

Um uns bis an die Zimmerdecke
sitzt die Welt
die Jahrhunderte auf den Regalen
ich frage dich oder du fragst
die Jahrhunderte spitzen die Ohren
Tiere im Zirkus
Ein Wink und sie springen
gehorsam geben sie Antwort

Alles was gelebt hat
was leben wird
antwortet dir
du antwortest mir
ringsum nicken sie uns zu
weil du da bist
und alle kennst
da ist keiner tot der gelebt hat
solange du bei mir bist

ANSWER

For E. W. P.[10]

The world sits around us
all the way to the room's ceiling
the centuries on the bookshelves
I ask you or you ask
the centuries sharpen the ears
animals in the circus
A nod and they jump
obediently they answer

Everything that has lived
that will live
answers you
you answer me
all around they nod to us
because you are here
and know all of them
here no one is dead who has lived
as long as you are with me

LEKTÜRE

Durch ein großes Tor
ziehn die Bücher in mich ein
sie zahlen etwas
bei ihrem Eintritt
sie geben etwas ab
bei meiner unsichtbaren Garderobiere

Das Theater
in das sie eintreten
ist dunkel
ich selber stehe am Eingang
die die ich liebe
ich weiß nicht wie sie herauskamen

kommen immer von neuem

READING

Books enter me
through a great gate
they pay something
when they come in
they leave something behind
with my invisible cloakroom attendant

The theater
in which they enter
is dark
I myself stand at the entrance
those whom I love
I don't know how they got out

come always anew

Einhorn

Die Freude
dieses bescheidenste Tier
dies sanfte Einhorn

so leise
man hört es nicht
wenn es kommt, wenn es geht
mein Haustier
Freude

wenn es Durst hat
leckt es die Tränen
von den Träumen.

UNICORN

The joy
of this humblest of animals
this gentle unicorn

so quiet
one doesn't hear it
when it comes, when it goes
my house-pet
joy

when it's thirsty
it licks the tears
from the dreams

Das Wachsen von Träumen

Das Wachsen von Träumen
macht Angst
als fehlten die Flügel
diese Mauern
zu überfliegen.

Schrei nach
einer Hand, einer Tür,
aus Fleisch, aus Holz.

THE GROWTH OF DREAMS

The growth of dreams
is frightening
as if missing wings
to fly over
these walls.

Cry out for
a hand, a door,
made of flesh, of wood.

WILLKÜRLICHE CHRONOLOGIE

Die Totenmaske jedes Tages
den du gelebt,
so ungleich geprägt
der Abdruck des Herzens.

Blicklose Tage
wie die Blinden
in den Straßen Sevillas.
Ketten von Blinden
an einem Stab.
Umsonst die Segel auf den Balkonen
Und auf den Dächern,
der Ruf zur Fahrt,
das helle Blau.
Wenn die Blinden kommen
eingesammelt an ihrem Stab,
nichts als Blinde
von einer Straßenseite zur andern.
Arme Blinde in Bastschuhn,
wenn Abend wird
und ein Kind genügt
für eine Schnur von Männern.

Tage wie Segel so hell,
so weiß in blau,
Leintücher für ein Bett
für einen oder zwei,
tanzend über den Häusern.
Das Haus,
die Straße,
der Tag,
alles fährt,
so leicht,

ARBITRARY CHRONOLOGY

The death-masks of each day
that you've lived,
so differently embossed
the imprint of the heart.

Unseeing days
like the blind
in the streets of Seville.
Lines of the blind
on a pole.
In vain the sails on the balconies
and on the roofs,
the call to the journey,
the bright blue.
When the blind come
gathered on their pole,
nothing but the blind
from one side of the street to the other.
Poor blind ones wearing straw sandals,
when evening comes
and a child suffices
for a cord of men.

Days like sails so bright,
so white on blue,
linen sheets for a bed
for one or two,
dancing above the houses.
The house,
the street,
the day,
everything journeys forth,
so easy,

so fremd, so vertraut,
so wach im Atem der Luft.
Ein Bettuch als Segel genügt
für jedes Schiff.

Tage
wie ein Hausflur so dunkel
wenn du hingefallen bist und es
sehr weh tut
und du sehr klein bist
und alle Klinken zu hoch
und keine Türe sich öffnet,
und niemand
dich bei der Hand nimmt.

Tage so blicklos und zögernd,
so schnell, so blau, so weiß,
so bitter wie die Orangen
an den Orangenbäumen Sevillas,
für die der Zucker
auf fernen Inseln wächst.

so strange, so familiar,
so alert in the breath of the air.
A bedsheet suffices as a sail
for every ship.

Days
like a hallway so dark
when you fell and it
hurt so badly
and you're very small
and all the door latches are too high
and no door opens,
and no one
takes you by the hand.

Days so unseeing and hesitant,
so quick, so blue, so white,
as bitter as the oranges
on the orange-trees of Seville,
for which the sugar
grows on distant islands.

ECCE HOMO

Weniger als die Hoffnung auf ihn

das ist der Mensch
einarmig
immer

Nur der gekreuzigte
beide Arme
weit offen
der Hier-Bin-Ich

Behold the Man[11]

Less than our hope in him

that is the human being
one-armed
always

Only the crucified
both arms
wide open
the Here-Am-I

INSELMITTAG

Wir sind Fremde
von Insel
zu Insel.
Aber am Mittag, wenn uns das Meer
bis ins Bett steigt
und die Vergangenheit
wie Kielwasser
an unsern Fersen abläuft
und das tote Meerkraut am Strand
zu goldenen Bäumen wird,
dann hält uns kein Netz
der Erinnerung mehr,
wir gleiten
hinaus,
und die abgesteckten
Meerstraßen der Fischer
und die Tiefenkarten
gelten nicht
für uns.

ISLAND NOON

We are strangers
from island
to island:
But at noon, when the sea
rises up to the bed
and the past
drains away
like a wake at our heels
and the dead seaweed on the beach
changes into golden trees,
then no net of memory
can hold us,
and we drift
out,
and the sea-routes fishermen
staked out
and the depth charts
don't apply
to us.

KALENDER

1
Grüne Pfennige
zittern
an den Birken.
Die Bäume binden sich kleine Wolken vor.
Die Vögel so aufgeregt
mit bebenden Kehlen.
Wer hier geblieben wäre
könnte das Leben
nach den Kastanienblüten zählen.

2
Die geprügelten Tage
die so zutraulich begannen.

Schon hängen die Früchte ins Fenster.
Gestern
die Dolden.

Einer
deiner Sommer.

3
Der Schmerz steigt wie ein großer Nebel hoch
und löscht
die Ränder der Jahre.

Calendar

1
Green pennies
tremble
on the birches.
The trees tie little clouds to themselves.
The birds so excited
with quivering throats.
Whoever would have remained here
could have counted
life by means of horse-chestnut blossoms.

2
The pummeled days
that began so trustingly.

Already the fruit hangs in the windows.
Yesterday
the umbels.

One of
your summers.

3
The pain rises up like a great fog
and extinguishes
the years' edges.

DIE FLÜGEL DER LERCHEN

Die Flügel der Lerchen
sind unnütz
sie sitzen geblendet
im Käfig
Beweise gegen uns

Unsre Rosen sind schwarz
geworden
im Regen
Unser Wein wird zu Essig
schon in der Kelter
und unsre Feste
zu Tagen der Prüfung

Aus den goldenen Füllhörnern
steigen die Maden
Giftige Wolken verdunkeln
den Himmel über den Städten
Es wäre Mut
Angst zu haben

The Larks' Wings

The larks' wings
are useless
they sit blinded
in the cage
Evidence against us

Our roses have
blackened
in the rain
Our wine turns to vinegar already
in the winepress
and our celebrations
become days of testing

Maggots climb
out of the golden cornucopias
Poisonous clouds darken
the sky above the cities
It would be courageous
to be afraid

WEIL VERLIEREN SO LEICHT IST

Der Ring mit dem hellblauen Stein
den dir ein Traum gegeben
du hast die Hand geöffnet
im Schlaf
da verlorst du den Ring
Kroch eine Schnecke hindurch
eine nackte Schnecke im Regen
und trug ihn in ihr schleimiges Erdloch
den Ring mit dem Traumstein?
Fiel er dir in den Brunnen
während du schliefst?

Du hast im Schlaf die Hand geöffnet
da verlorst du den Ring
wie du alles verlierst
—wie wir alle alles verlieren—
Tag um Tag,
was wir haben verlieren
weil verlieren so leicht ist
nur verloren haben
so schwer
Weil mühsam ist
bewahren was wir lieben
mühsam wir selbst zu sein

Doch ohne den Mut
die Hand in der Hand zu halten
ohne den Mut
ganz hier zu sein
werden wir täglich
ärmer

Because Losing Is So Easy

The ring with the bright-blue stone
which gave you a dream
you opened your hand
in your sleep
then lost the ring
Did a snail crawl by
a naked snail in the rain
and did it carry it into its slimy hole in the ground
the ring with the dream-stone?
Did it fall into the fountain
while you slept?

As you slept you opened your hand
then lost the ring
just as you lose everything
—like we all lose everything—
day after day,
what we have we lose
because losing is so easy
but to have lost
so hard
Because it's strenuous
to watch over what we love
strenuous to be ourselves

Yet without the courage
to hold hand in hand
without the courage
to be utterly here
we become daily
poorer

Mein Herze wir sind verreist

Für E. W. P.

Mein Herze
wir sind verreist
nach verschiedenen Weltteilen
Eurydike
meine Hand
deine Schulter berührend
Ich schreibe mit deinem Stift
ich möchte eintreten
durch diese großen Trichter
am Meer
in das Reich
in dem du gehst oder liegst
oder stehst
in dem du jetzt alles weißt
oder alles vergißt

Ich dein schneller dein zu langsamer
Weggefährte
Ich komme hinter dir her
‚Langsamer‘ sagst du wie immer
‚Sei langsam‘

So sitze ich hier
hoch über dem Meer
blau grün fern
deinen Stift in der Hand

My Heart, We've Set Forth

For E. W. P.[12]

My heart
we've set forth
for various parts of the world
Eurydice
my hand
touching your shoulder
I write with your pen
I'd like to come in
through this great crater
in the sea
into the kingdom
in which you walk or lie
or stand
in which you now know everything
or forget everything

I your speedy your too slow
companion
I follow behind you
"Slower" you always say
"Be slow"

So I sit here
high above the sea
blue green distant
your pen in my hand

SCHLIMMES BÜNDNIS

Wir verbünden uns mit der Zeit
dieser Abschöpferin
aller Freude
‚Hier hast du nimm‘
Und sie nimmt

Sie ist sehr groß
im Nehmen

Sie ist sehr groß
im Lassen
Sie gönnt uns
ungeschmälert
die Tränen

A Terrible Alliance

We form an alliance with time
this destroyer
of all joy
"Here you have it take"
And time takes

It is very large
in taking

It is very large
in leaving
It grants us
tears
undiminished

GLEICHGEWICHT

Wir gehen
jeder für sich
den schmalen Weg
über den Köpfen der Toten
—fast ohne Angst—
im Takt unsres Herzens,
als seien wir beschützt,
solange die Liebe
nicht aussetzt.

So gehen wir
zwischen Schmetterlingen und Vögeln
in staunendem Gleichgewicht
zu einem Morgen von Baumwipfeln
—grün, gold und blau—
und zu dem Erwachen
der geliebten Augen.

Equilibrium

We walk
each for themselves
the narrow way
over the heads of the dead
—almost fearlessly—
to the beat of our heart
as if we were protected,
as long as love
doesn't fail us.

We walk like this
between butterflies and birds
in an astonishing equilibrium
to a morning of treetops
—green, gold and blue—
and to the awakening
of beloved eyes.

UNAUFHALTSAM

Das eigene Wort,
wer holt es zurück,
das lebendige
eben noch ungesprochene
Wort?

Wo das Wort vorbeifliegt
verdorren die Gräser,
werden die Blätter gelb,
fällt Schnee.
Ein Vogel käme dir wieder.
Nicht dein Wort,
das eben noch ungesagte,
in deinen Mund.
Du schickst andere Worte
hinterdrein,
Worte mit bunten, weichen Federn.
Das Wort ist schneller,
das schwarze Wort.
Es kommt immer an,
es hört nicht auf, an-
zukommen.

Besser ein Messer als ein Wort.
Ein Messer kann stumpf sein.
Ein Messer trifft oft
am Herzen vorbei.
Nicht das Wort.
Am Ende ist das Wort,
immer
am Ende
das Wort.

Unstoppable

One's own word,
who takes it back,
the living
yet still unspoken
word?

Where the word flies by
the grasses wither,
the leaves yellow,
snow falls.
A bird might come to you again.
Not so your word,
the one yet unsaid,
in your mouth.
You send other words
after it,
words with colorful, soft feathers.
The word is faster,
the black word.
It always arrives,
it never stops
arriving.

Better a knife than a word.
A knife can be dull.
A knife often misses
the heart.
Not the word.
In the end is the word,
always
in the end
the word.

Morgens und abends

1
Immer wieder die schwarzen Vögel
über mich wegfliegend.
Diese Frühaufsteher,
wenn ich die Augen öffne.

Und des Abends
—ich zu müd mich zu wehren—
ein verspäteter,
der in meinem Haar übernachtet.

2
Die Wiesen, die Augen
früh und spät
so naß.

Dazwischen
ist Tag.

Mornings and Evenings

1
Again and again the black birds
above me flying away.
These early risers,
when I open my eyes.

And at eventide
—I too tired to defend myself—
a late one
who spends the night in my hair.

2
The meadows, the eyes
early and late
so damp.

Day lies
between.

KNOSPE

Die Knospe einer Liebkosung,
von keinem Gärtner gepflegt,
im Laub meines Körpers verborgen,
langsam,
unaufhaltsam sich öffnend,
macht mich fremd mit mir selbst.

Bud

The bud of a caress,
tended by no gardener,
hidden in the foliage of my body,
slowly,
inexorably opening itself,
estranges me from myself.

HARZEND

Die immer frische Wunde der Kiefern
die nie verjährt
dieser weinende Wald
voller Tränenbecher
Das Messer das erinnert
und nichts heilen läßt

Die Zeit
wird die grünen Haare trocknen
nicht die Wunde

Diese nackten
Stämme
sollten Kleider tragen dürfen

Resinous

The ever-fresh wound of the pine
that never ages
this weeping forest
filled with cups of tears
The knife that remembers
and lets nothing heal

Time
will dry the green hair
not the wound

The naked
trunks
should be allowed to wear clothes

Haus ohne Fenster

Der Schmerz sargt uns ein
in einem Haus ohne Fenster.
Die Sonne, die die Blumen öffnet,
zeigt seine Kanten
nur deutlicher.
Es ist ein Würfel aus Schweigen
in der Nacht.

Der Trost,
der keine Fenster findet und keine Türen
und hinein will,
trägt erbittert das Reisig zusammen.
Er will ein Wunder erzwingen
und zündet es an,
das Haus aus Schmerz.

WINDOWLESS HOUSE

Pain entombs us
in a windowless house.
The sun which opens the flowers
shows pain's edges
ever more clearly.
It's a dice made of silence
in the night.

The comfort
that finds no windows and no doors
and wants to come in
bitterly gathers the brushwood together.
It wants to force a miracle
and ignites it,
this house of pain.

RUFE NICHT

Lege den Finger auf den Mund.
Rufe nicht.
Bleibe stehen
am Wegrand.
Vielleicht solltest du dich hinlegen
in den Staub.
Dann siehst du in den Himmel
und bist eins mit der Straße,
und wer sich umdreht nach dir
kann gehen als lasse er niemand zurück.
Es geht sich leichter fort,
wenn du liegst als wenn du stehst,
wenn du schweigst als wenn du rufst.
Sieh die Wolken ziehn.
Sei bescheiden, halte nichts fest.
Sie lösen sich auf.
Auch du bist sehr leicht.
Auch du wirst nicht dauern.
Es lohnt sich nicht Angst zu haben
vor Verlassenheit,
wenn schon der Wind steigt
der die Wolke
verweht.

Don't Call

Lay your finger on your mouth.
Don't call.
Stay put
on the path's edge.
Perhaps you should lie down
in the dust.
Then you'd look at the sky
and be one with the street,
and whoever turns toward you
can go as if he'd left no one behind.
It is easier to leave
when you lie down than when you stand,
when you keep silent than when you call.
Watch the clouds drift.
Be humble, hold nothing fast.
They'll break apart.
Even you are quite light.
Even you won't endure.
It's not worth being afraid
of abandonment
when the wind is already rising
which blows
the cloud away.

MEIN GESCHLECHT ZITTERT

Mein Geschlecht zittert
wie ein Vögelchen
unter dem Griff deines Blicks.

Deine Hände eine zärtliche Brise
auf meinem Leib.
Alle meine Wachen fliehn.

Du öffnest die letzte Tür.
Ich bin so erschrocken
vor Glück
daß aller Schlaf dünn wird
wie ein zerschlissenes Tuch.

My Sex Trembles

My sex trembles
like a little bird
in the grasp of your gaze.

Your hands a tender breeze
on my body.
I drop my guard entirely.

You open the last door.
I'm so shocked
with joy
that sleep becomes as thin
as a threadbare scarf.

RUF

Mich ruft der Gärtner.

Unter der Erde seine Blumen
sind blau.

Tief unter der Erde
seine Blumen
sind blau.

CALL

The gardener calls me.

Beneath the earth his flowers
are blue.

Deep beneath the earth
his flowers
are blue.

IMMER KREISEN

Immer kreisen
auf dem kühleren Wind
hilflos

kreisen meine Worte
heimwehgefiedert
nestlos

einst einem Lächeln entgegen
keiner trägt das Leben allein
kreisend und kreisend.

Always Circling

Always circling
on cooler wind
helplessly

my words circle
feathered with homesickness
nestless

once toward a laugh
no one bears life alone
circling and circling.

Versprechen an eine Taube

Taube,
ich suchte einen Tisch
da find ich
dich,
Taube,
auf dem Rücken liegend
die rosa Füße an den hellen Leib gepreßt
abgestürzt
aus dem Licht,
Botin,
in einen Trödelladen.

Taube,
wenn mein Haus verbrennt
wenn ich wieder verstoßen werde
wenn ich alles verliere
dich nehme ich mit,
Taube aus wurmstichigem Holz,
wegen des sanften Schwungs
deines einzigen
ungebrochenen
Flügels.

Promise for a Dove

Dove,
I was looking for a table
and found
you,
dove,
lying on your back
the pink feet pressed on the bright body
crashed down
out of the light,
messenger,
in a second-hand shop.

Dove,
when my house burned
when I will be expelled again
when I lose everything
you I take with me,
dove made of wood-wormed wood,
because of the soft swaying
of your own one
unbroken
wing.

Ich setzte den Fuß in die Luft,
und sie trug.[13]

I stepped into the air,
and it carried me.

Hilde Domin

NOTES

All poems included in this collection are from Hilde Domin's *Sämtliche Gedichte*, edited by Nikola Herweg and Melanie Reinhold, with an afterword by Ruth Klüger (S. Fischer Verlag, 2009), and all citations of Domin's poems refer to translations in *The Wandering Radiance*. All translations from Domin's essays and other writings are by Mark S. Burrows.

NOTE ON THE EPIGRAPH

1. "The Saints," 217.

NOTES ON THE FOREWORD

1. *Why Poetry Still Today?* is a play on the title Domin gave to a collection of essays on poetics, *Why Poetry Today* (*Wozu Lyrik Heute. Dichtung und Leser in der gesteuerten Gesellschaft*; R. Piper & Co. Verlag, 1971); see also *xxviii–xxix*.
2. "This Wide Wing," 139.
3. Born Hildegard Dina Löwenstein, she married Erwin Walter Palm in 1936 and only later took the surname Domin as a *nom de plume* to express her gratitude to the nation that had offered them refuge during the 1940s and early 50s. See *xxi* and *xxiii*.
4. This phrase is taken from her essay „*Unter Akrobaten und Vögeln*" in *Gesammelte autobiographische Schriften. Fast ein Lebenslauf* (S. Fischer Verlag, 1993), 21.
5. This phrase is the epigraph for the second section of Domin's first collection of poems, *Nur eine Rose als Stütze* (S. Fischer Verlag, 1959); reprinted in *Sämtliche Gedichte*, 47.
6. "Wish", 173.
7. For a discussion of the origin of this book, see *xxvi*.
8. „*Asternfeld*" in *Sämtliche Gedichte*, 98–99.
9. From a letter dated March 25, 1959.
10. Marion Tauschwitz shares this episode in her biography of Hilde Domin, *Hilde Domin. Dass ich sein kann wie ich bin* (zu Klampen, 2015), 14.
11. The phrase "*magische Gebrauchsgegenstände*" is one Domin coined in an early autobiographical essay and returned to in her later Frankfurt Lectures on Poetics (1987–88); see *xxix–xxxiii*.
12. „*Tröstung*" in *Sämtliche Gedichte*, 220–21.
13. „*Bei der Lektüre Pablo Nerudas*" in *Sämtliche Gedichte*, 129.

1. *„Offener Brief an Nelly Sachs. Zur Frage der Exildichtung"* (1966); later published in *Gesammelte autobiographische Schriften*, 175.
2. *„Unter Akrobaten und Vögeln. Fast ein Lebenslauf"* ("Among Acrobats and Birds: Almost a Life-Sketch"). Domin wrote this essay in 1962, later publishing it in *Besondere Kennzeichen*, edited by Karl Ude (List Verlag, 1964); see also *Gesammelte autobiographische Schriften*, 21–31.
3. See note 13.
4. *Gesammelte autobiographische Schriften*, 21.
5. "Among Acrobats and Birds" is a phrase borrowed from the title poem of her first collection, *Nur eine Rose als Stütze*.
6. "Only a Rose for Support," 11.
7. "A Different Birth," 9; see also note 13.
8. *Gesammelte autobiographische Schriften*, 21–22.
9. A translation of *Geborgenheit* with any single English word lacks the overtones that belong to the rich and complex experience this word connotes. The root of the word, *"bergen,"* could be rendered as "to save" or even "to rescue," which echoed the literal experience undergirding Domin's use of the word. For the poem she wrote with this as its title, see 206.
10. See "Exile and Homeland," *xxxviii–xli*. Domin echoed this theme in her later poem "Five Songs for Leaving the Country," 225.
11. *„Unter Akrobaten und Vögeln"* in *Gesammelte autobiographische Schriften*, 21. For the reference to being *vaterlandslos*, see her poem "Fatherlands," 43.
12. *„Offener Brief an Nelly Sachs. Zur Frage der Exildichtung"* (1966); later published in *Gesammelte autobiographische Schriften*, 175
13. Domin explores the theme of *"die zweite Chance"* ("the second chance") in the fifth lecture of her Frankfurt Lectures in Poetics, entitled *„Sisyphos: die tägliche Anstrengung das Unmögliche zu tun. – Der schreibende Asylant als Sonderfall der Sisyphosexistenz. – Das Postulat der zweiten Chance: der Neubeginn"* ("Sisyphus: the daily exertion of doing the impossible. – The writing asylum-seeker as a special example of Sisyphus' existence. The postulate of the 'second chance': the new beginning"). These lectures were published as *Das Gedicht als Augenblick von Freiheit. Frankfurter Poetik-Vorlesungen* 1987–88 (S. Fischer Verlag, 1993), 85–101.
14. *„R.A. Bauer interviewt Hilde Domin 1972 in Heidelberg"* in *Gesammelte autobiographische Schriften*, 248.
15. Ibid, 244.
16. This phrase came in a letter she had written to her husband which she later added as the epigraph to her first published book; see *Sämtliche Gedichte*, 47.
17. In a later essay of 1974, entitled *„Meine Wohnungen—'Mis moradas'"* ("My Homes—My Dwellings"), she described it as *"ein sehr bürgerliches Haus,"* in contrast to the places she lived during the decades of her exile: "Most of the

apartments in which I have lived were apartments for those in flight or for refugees, or they were suddenly changed from what seemed to be entirely normal dwellings. That stays in one's bones for one's entire life." *Gesammelte autobiographische Schriften*, 71–72.

18. Cited by Ruth Klüger, „*Nachwort*" in *Sämtliche Gedichte*, 307.

19. Hilde Domin, *Gesammelte Essays: Heimat in der Sprache* (*Collected Essays: A Homeland in Language*; S. Fischer Verlag, 1993), 5. She had earlier written a tender essay to express her devotion to her father, entitled „*Mein Vater. Wie ich ihn erinnere*" ("My Father. As I remember him"), in *Gesammelte autobiographische Schriften*, 10–20. She concluded that piece with this poignant observation: "It is certainly much easier to think on a father who was persecuted and whose life was destroyed, rather than on one who was a persecutor. Or one who watched, or looked away, as others were persecuted. One who was persecuted has one advantage over the others: he is excused from the dilemma of responsibility. His defenselessness is complete," 20.

20. Cited in Tauschwitz, *Hilde Domin. Das ich sein kann wie ich bin*, 50.

21. "On the Clouds' Guarantee," 77.

22. In an early autobiographical essay first published in 1964, Domin remarked that "as it turned out, my husband found himself in a second marriage with me. With me, a person who still cooked following the same recipes and whose soufflés had not suffered [from this change], and who still enjoyed sleeping in until 9 a.m. Otherwise, however, everything [about me] had changed. Before then, I was round and ample, but now I am slender. Earlier, I planned, but now every day is only today, and in the morning, the evening seems unimaginably distant. I, so useful, have become unuseful. And, worst of all, I am a son who turned everything upside down. Who requires great patience and whom one would sometimes like to throw out. Each breath of mine is that of an *enfant terrible*. But this is not my fault, it has to do with the fact that I have come into the world with a bang." See „*Unter Akrobaten und Vögeln*" in *Gesammelte autobiographische Schriften*, 29.

23. With the exception of twenty-two of these poems, published posthumously as *Gedichte aus dem Nachlaß* (*Unpublished Poems*) in the collection celebrating what would have been her one-hundredth birthday in 2009, most of these were never published—and, in any event, did not survive. Domin described this experience in an autobiographical essay written in 1959, when she observed that "after the death of my mother, about which I have nothing here to say, I came to a border and suddenly found the language I had long served. I came to know what a word meant. I freed myself through language. Had I not freed myself, I would no longer be living. I wrote poems. I wrote, naturally, in German. And as soon as I'd written them, I translated them into Spanish in order to see what they could withstand as texts. In order to find a proper distance [toward them]. I did not even consider publishing them. Writing was [my] salvation. I was thirty-nine years old when my life, as if of its own accord, became a pre-history

for the second life that I have since lived." See „Leben als Sprachodyssee" ("Life as Language-Odyssey") in *Gesammelte autobiographische Schriften*, 33.

24. "Allowed to Land," 13. This is an early, previously unpublished poem that Domin later included in her *Gesammelte Gedichte* (*Collected Poems*) of 1987.

25. "Pulling Landscape," 15.

26. Domin first published this lengthy poem, originally written in 1953, in the journal *Neue Rundschau* in 1957; see *Sämtliche Gedichte*, 275–82. It later appeared without the opening two stanzas in her first published volume, *Nur eine Rose als Stütze* (1959), the basis for the citation included here. The later revision, the third and final version, appeared in *Sämtliche Gedichte*, 221–27. The earliest form, eliminated in both later versions, opens with a brooding tone: "What perverse / sort of fear / cuts our clothing / from the skin of a 'you' / as if it were an animal pelt in winter? // The crow / has no fear of another crow / but the human / is the most fearful encounter / of human encounters. // The one it affects / will be lifted up," etc. In *Sämtliche Gedichte*, 275. Both later versions open with these lines: "The one whom it concerns / will be lifted up / as if by a huge crane / and set down / where nothing more is valid, / where no street / leads from yesterday to tomorrow..." Beyond these shared lines, these two later versions have a similar tone but with many alterations, from the original version and when compared to each other. See *Sämtliche Gedichte*, 38.

27. Tauschwitz, *Hilde Domin*, 262–64.

28. „Gefährlicher Löffel" in *Sämtliche Gedichte*, 228–29.

29. "Return," 115.

30. „Randbemerkungen zur Rückkehr" in *Gesammelte autobiographische Schriften*, 335, 338.

31. Domin later described her "first encounter with my publisher" in a short essay written in 1965–66, suggesting that a publisher is "a cross between a typewriter and a marriage partner," going on to recall José Ortega y Gasset's description of such love as "a connection of mutual admiration"; see „Erste Begegnung mit meinem Verleger" in *Gesammelte autobiographische Schriften*, 224. She dedicated the poem "The Hardest Ways," 73, to Hirsch; it was included in her debut collection, *Only a Rose for Support*.

32. Tauschwitz, *Hilde Domin*, 317.

33. Domin designated her birth year in that volume as 1912 so that the volume would appear to be the work of a forty-seven-year-old poet, rather than that of the fifty-year-old she actually was. See Tauschwitz, *Hilde Domin*, 350. Several later volumes, including—strangely—the Vita appendix to her *Gesammelte autobiographische Schriften* (345), include that false date.

34. Walter Jens, „Vollkommenheit im Einfachen. Eine Lyrikerin, die zu warten verstand, stellt sich vor" ("Perfection in Plainness. A poet who understood to wait introduces herself") in *Die Zeit* 48 (Nov. 27, 1959); this was Jens' contribution to the regular column "My Book of the Month." https://www.zeit.de/1959/48/vollkommenheit-im-einfachen; accessed on July 27, 2022.

35. Hans-Georg Gadamer, „*Hilde Domin, Dichterin der Rückkehr*" in *Vokabular der Erinnerungen. Zum Werk von Hilde Domin*, Bettina von Wangenheim and Ilseluise Metz, eds. (Fischer Verlag, 1998), 29–35; see also his essay „*Lieder zur Ermutigung II*" in *Heimkehr ins Wort. Materialien zu Hilde Domin*, Wangenheim and Metz, eds. (Fischer Verlag, 1982), 165–68.

36. See *Vokabular der Erinnerungen*, 13–28.

37. For a list of these awards, see Tauschwitz, „*Auszeichnungen und Preise*" in *Hilde Domin*, 585–86.

38. Ulla Hahn, „*Zum ‚Friedrich-Hölderlin-Preis'*" in *Vokabular der Erinnerungen*, 167–83 and „*Wortritt durch die Wüste*" in *Frankfurter Allgemeine Zeitung* (July 27, 2004).

39. See his remarks in „*Außerhalb der Regel*" ("Beyond the Rules") in *Vokabular der Erinnerungen*, 176–83.

40. Vera-Sabine Winkler, *Leise Bekenntnisse. Die Bedeutung der Poesie für die Sprache der Liturgie am Beispiel von Hilde Domin* (Matthias-Grünewald-Verlag, 2009), 52.

41. Ben Hutchinson, "Only a rose," a review of Ilka Schneidgen's *Hilde Domin. Dichterin des Dennoch* in *Times Literary Supplement* n. 5408 (Nov. 24, 2006); he is here citing lines from the poem „*Der Baum blüht trotzdem*" ("The Tree Blooms Regardless"); for my slightly different translation, see 143. In the course of his review, Hutchinson—himself an academic, it should be pointed out—remarks that Domin, who was "never a purely 'literary' poet,…has enjoyed a popularity with the common reader that induces suspicion among academics. The very virtues of her poetry, its clarity and affecting simplicity, are for some observers its principal vices."

42. *Das zweite Paradies. Roman in Segmenten* (*The Second Paradise. A Novel in Segments*), first published in 1968 by Piper Verlag.

43. For a retrospective essay written to commemorate Domin upon the publication in 2009 of Tauschwitz's biography, *Hilde Domin*, Domin's *Sämtliche Gedichte*, and *Die Liebe im Exil: Briefe an Erwin Walter Palm aus den Jahren 1931–1959*, edited by Jan Bürger and Frank Druffner (Fischer, 2009), Hutchinson points out that "by the time of her death, Domin had become a modern classic in Germany, taught in schools and beloved by readers who might not otherwise know much modern poetry. Her burial in Heidelberg approached the status of a state funeral, with, among others, the Minister for Culture giving a speech in which she mourned the loss not only for Heidelberg but also for the national culture more generally." See "*‚Dichterin der Rückkehr'*: Hilde Domin in Retrospect. A Review Article" in *Modern Language Review* 105:2 (April, 2010), 479–86.

44. For a full list of these prizes, awards, and distinctions, see Tauschwitz, „*Auszeichnungen und Preise*" in *Hilde Domin*, 585–86.

45. *Wozu Lyrik heute. Dichtung und Leser in der gesteuerten Gesellschaft*. The word "*wozu*" could be rendered "why" or "for what use."

46. Ibid, 17. She returned to this theme in her later *Das Gedicht als Augenblick von Freiheit*; see 18–22.

47. See *Gesammelte autobiographische Schriften*, 21. For details about her reception at these lectures, see Tauschwitz, *Hilde Domin*, 490–91.

48. *Das Gedicht als Augenblick von Freiheit*, 9.

49. Ibid.

50. Ibid., 7–8.

51. Domin began her first lecture by quoting the last part of the poem "Save Us," 155.

52. *Das Gedicht als Augenblick von Freiheit*, 18–19.

53. Ibid., 69.

54. Ibid. The phrase she used here is distinctive, quoting an uncited phrase: "*Das Gedicht ist, wie der Mensch selbst, ,eine wandelnde Vereinigung des Unvereinbaren,' ein Spannungsfeld seiner Möglichkeiten.*"

55. Ibid., 80. In an undated letter to Helmut Viebrok, she described her commitment to "nevertheless" as directed "against the fatal 'no-future' panic [of the day]"; see Tauschwitz, *Hilde Domin*, 491.

56. „*Unter Akrobaten und Vögeln,*" 28; see also *Das Gedicht als Augenblick von Freiheit*, 71.

57. "Pulling Landscape," 15.

58. *Das Gedicht als Augenblick von Freiheit*, 72–73. Hugo was banished from France following the coup-d'etat by Louis Napoleon Bonaparte in December, 1851, and later expelled both from Belgium in 1852 and Jersey in 1855 before finding refuge in Guernsey in October of that year. It is no wonder that Domin felt a deep affinity with his plight as one forced into exile.

59. From a section entitled „*Lieder zur Ermutigung*" or "Songs of Encouragement" in *Rückkehr der Schiffe*; in *Sämtliche Gedichte*, 108.

60. *Das Gedicht als Augenblick von Freiheit*, 72.

61. "Among Acrobats and Birds" in *Gesammelte autobiographische Schriften*, 30.

62. "Who Could Do It," 67; *Das Gedicht als Augenblick von Freiheit*, 85.

63. *Gesammelte autobiographische Schriften*, 25.

64. Ibid., 29–30. She later elaborated on this theme in the third of her Frankfurt Lectures on Poetics; see *Das Gedicht als Augenblick von Freiheit*, 57–58.

65. *Das Gedicht als Augenblick von Freiheit*, 52.

66. See *xxvii*.

67. „*Ratschlag für Abiturienten*" in *Gesammelte Essays*, 254–55.

68. Ibid.

69. „*Schiff ohne Hafen. Aufruf zur Rettung der Vietnamflüchtlinge,*" 23 (Nov. 1978); in *Gesammelte Essays*, 304–7.

70. "The Hardest Ways," 73.

71. "Between Always and Always," 5.

72. "Don't Grow Weary," 3.

73. *Das Gedicht als Augenblick von Freiheit*, 99–100.

74. "Retreat," 87.
75. *Das Gedicht als Augenblick von Freiheit,* 51.

NOTE ON "EXILE AND HOMELAND"

1. This essay is taken in lightly abridged form from the *„Vorwort"* ("Foreword") and opening essay, *„Heimat"* ("Homeland"), in *Gesammelte Essays,* 11–16.

NOTES ON THE POEMS

1. Domin employs the verb *"erlöschen"*—which means "to extinguish"—in a deliberate manner here. When she uses it as a noun—das Erlöschen—the force of the word means something more than "the extinguishing" and something closer to "extinction." I have chosen to render her use of the gerund *"Er-löschender"* as "one burning out," a choice that fails to bring across the verbal echo she intends with *"das Erlöschen,"* however, when it appears in this stanza. One might render *"das Erlöschen"* as "burnout," though this carries an unintended (and therefore misleading) overtone in colloquial English that is alien to the poet's intent. It must also be said that the choice to render *"Erlöschender"* as "one burning out" suggests a more direct reference to Domin's choice of the imperative verb *"brenne"* ("burn") in the second stanza, though the parallel in the actions described is clear.
2. Domin published this poem in two versions; I have drawn on the first version, published in the collection entitled *Ich will dich* (1970/1995) and later published in a form that included only Part I in *Gesammelte Gedichte* (1987). The first line ends with the verb *"aufgehoben,"* the past participle of the word *"aufheben,"* a word that can be used in contradictory ways—meaning "to lift up" but also "to cancel" or "abolish." It is also a word Hegel often used to describe the dialectic process of "sublation"—i.e., to lift something to a higher level in a transcending manner.
3. Domin's choice of the phrase *"das Herz eine Kugel / gestoßen / einen Zentimeter rollend"* suggests the sport of shotput (*Kugelstoß*), as if the heart could be "hurled" (or "put") like a heavy metal ball (or "shot"), but because of its weight it would only roll a very short distance. She then reverses directions in the final stanza, portraying the heart as a "great hurler / of all balls."
4. This poem is taken from Domin's last collection *Der Baum blüht trotzdem*; a poem with the same title appeared in her first book, *Nur eine Rose als Stütze;* see *Sämtliche Gedichte,* 15–16.
5. All of these writers were Jewish survivors of the Holocaust who took their lives in the decades that followed. Paul Celan (born Paul Antschel) was a Jewish Romanian-born, German-language poet whose parents died in a Roma-

nian internment camp; he was also incarcerated in a work-camp and, after the war, emigrated to France where he became a French citizen, later dying by drowning in the Seine on April 20, 1970. Péter Szondi survived interment at the concentration camp Bergen-Belsen before being released; he later became a professor at the Free University of Berlin, and committed suicide in 1971 by drowning himself, leaving unfinished a book exploring the writings of his friend Paul Celan. Jean Améry (born Hanns Chaim Mayer) survived torture at the hands of the German Gestapo and later imprisonment in the concentration camps in Auschwitz, Buchenwald, and finally Bergen-Belsen where he was released at the war's end in 1945; he died by suicide in 1978 of an overdose. All three struggled with surviving in the face of so many who did not; in Amery's book *At the Mind's Limits: Contemplations by a Survivor on Auschwitz and Its Realities* (1966), he argued that torture was "the essence" of the Third Reich.

6. "Save us from the lion's mouth," Psalm 22:21 (the citation from the Vulgate follows a different numeration: Psalm 21:22).

7. The title of this poem, „Talfahrt," literally means a "valley drive" or "drive into the valley." This word is generally rendered as "descent" in English, but it has the figurative meaning of "decline," which the poem's intent suggests.

8. This title, „Ars Longa," literally "long art," echoes the Latin maxim, "ars longa, vita brevis"—that is, "art is long, life short."

9. Christa Wolf (1929–2011) was an East German writer whose family had been expelled from a region that became part of Poland after World War II. *Patterns of Childhood*, published in 1976, was one of her best-known novels, exploring themes of exile and what Germans refer to as *Vergangenheitsbewälti-gung*, the work of "overcoming the past"—that is, the inner process of coming to terms with one's past—in this case both the Nazi past Wolf had known in her "homeland" in what had been part of eastern Prussia, and that of the totalitar- ian state where she grew up after the war. The novel's basic narrative and many of its details are largely autobiographical dimensions.

10. E. W. P. are the initials of Domin's husband, Erwin Walter Palm.

11. This is the Latin version of Pilate's words when he presented Jesus to the crowd shortly before he was crucified; see John 19:5.

12. Dedicated to her husband, Erwin Walter Palm.

13. See *Sämtliche Gedichte*, 47.

INDEX

TITLES IN ENGLISH

ACKNOWLEDGMENTS

This book, like many, has had a long gestation, and I am grateful to acknowledge those whose contributions helped usher it into life. My first encounter with Hilde Domin's poems was a long time in coming. Since my college years I have been an avid reader of German poetry, and eventually majored in German literature as an undergraduate at Lawrence University. For reasons I cannot explain, however, I did not at the time come upon her poems—or even her name. Had I been an "English-only" reader, this might have been understandable since her poetry at the time was largely untouched by English translators. But that was not the case. I arrived at the university as a bilingual student with interests in modern German literature, and while I'd taken advanced seminars on modern German poets, Domin's works were not included. When I later moved to Tübingen under the auspices of a Fulbright Fellowship for graduate studies, I had turned my attention to philosophy and theology. I did hear lectures by Prof. Walter Jens, the first literary critic to review Domin's writings, but at the time his focus was elsewhere.

The decisive encounter came the year after Hilde Domin's death, in 2007. That year I had an appointment as guest professor at the *Kirchliche Hochschule*, a graduate theological school in Wuppertal, Germany. I had long known about this school, established in 1934 as a seminary of the "Confessing Church" (*Bekennende Kirche*). From the outset this was a confessional movement of resistance against the "Aryan" policies of the Nazis, which had been zealously embraced by a larger faction within the Protestant Church, the so-called *Deutsche Christen* ("German Christians"). This school only survived for a few years—under duress—until Himmler closed it in August, 1937; it continued "underground" for several more years before disbanding in 1941. The school reopened in the fall of 1945, a sign of hope in the dark and difficult years after the war; by the time I arrived there, the faculty had established a strong commitment to cultivating Jewish-Christian relations. Domin would have found a warm welcome there.

In one sense she did, if in an indirect manner. During that year, Prof. Dr. Günter Ruddat invited me to attend the *Sozietät* in Practical Theology, a postgraduate seminar that met periodically to discuss current research projects by faculty members and postgraduate students. In a session of that *Sozietät*, I had the good fortune of meeting Prof. Ruddat's doctoral student, Vera-Sabine Winkler, who was writing a dissertation exploring Domin's writings in terms of "liturgical poetics." Several years later, in the centenary of Domin's birth, she published the fruit of that research, *Leise Bekenntnisse. Die Bedeu-*

tung der Poesie für die Sprache der Liturgie am Beispiel von Hilde Domin (Matthias-Grünewald-Verlag, 2009). I am grateful to Vera for that engaged and thoughtful introduction to Domin, for her longstanding interest in my work on poetics, and for her support of this book as it took shape over the last decade.

From the start, I found myself drawn by Domin's voice, even though I also found myself often puzzled by her abbreviated diction and at times eccentric syntax—all falling under the wide umbrella of poetic license, to be sure. I sensed, though, that I was in the presence of a writer—à la Emily Dickinson—who knew to "Tell all the Truth but tell it slant," trusting her readers to discover that "Success in Circuit lies." After meeting Vera and encountering Domin's work, I found my way to a bookshop in Wuppertal and bought a copy of *Nur eine Rose als Stütze*, Domin's first collection, from the imprint of December, 2006—which had a print-run by then of 46–53 thousand! Thus began my long courtship with her poems, and theirs with me. I rarely underscore lines in poetry collections out of respect for the uncluttered page, but this was an exception: I see now that I had marked, if discreetly, the lines that appear as the epigraph to this volume: *"Denn wir essen Brot, / aber wir leben von Glanz"* ("For we eat bread, but we live from radiance"). How could any reader not become enchanted by a claim like this? I at least sought no defense against their lure.

What I found remarkable from the outset was the distinctive voice woven through her poems. Sometimes they seemed to speak in an intimate whisper, at other times with abrupt bursts of excitement. And I could immediately sense something of what they seemed to be steering toward, even if their reach often exceeded my grasp. Such is the nature of strong poems like hers. Under the spell of their allurement, I found myself drawn by the strange weave of unexpected images and startling phrases they carried. That experience, with all its attraction, has only grown over the years.

Later that year, I found myself the guest of Dr. Ingrid Eisolt, the mother of my wife's brother-in-law, at her home in Cologne. A retired medical doctor, she had spent much of her professional life in that city and had a long devotion to literature and the arts. As it happened, I noticed a copy of Domin's *Sämtliche Gedichte* on her bookshelf, a volume that had been published earlier that year; as we talked about our common interest in this *kölnische Dichterin*, or "Cologne poet," she took down her copy and gave it to me. "These poems will take you on a long journey," she said, little knowing how true that would be.

Momentum for this project gathered in 2012 when I applied for, and received, the Wytter Bynner Prize in Poetry. That generous fellowship included an art-residency at the Santa Fe Art Institute, and in my application for this grant I stated my intent to translate a collection of Domin's poems. That work began during the residency that followed, in the late summer of 2013. I am glad to acknowledge the Wytter Bynner Foundation for Poetry and the SFAI for their support of this project in its early stages. That residency, as it turned out, gathered an extraordinarily diverse community of artists whose interest in my work turned out to be as generous as it was substantive. The response on the part of the audience that gathered for the public talk I gave about this work was a further affirmation, bolstering my conviction that Domin would find a warm reception among English readers.

Earlier that year I had moved to Germany to accept a professorship at the Protestant University of Applied Sciences in Bochum, and over the course of that decade I found myself among faculty colleagues and students who welcomed my work on poetics. Among them, Prof. Dr. Gotthard Fermor bears special mention. We shared a common passion for the poetry of Rainer Maria Rilke, which led to my joining the "Bonn Rilke Projekt" in the winter of 2013; that "project" produced a new three-volume publication, under Gotthard's editorship, of Rilke's *Book of Hours* (Gütersloh/Random House), and we took this project on tour as a performance-event over the next six years in cities and towns across Germany. Gotthard had also long been a student of Domin's poetry, and our conversations about her work deepened my appreciation of the distinctive place she occupied in German literature and culture.

Over the last decade I have often found myself drawing on Domin's poems—in my own largely unpublished translations, in academic lectures, as well as workshops and retreats I've led for popular audiences around the world: in England, Scotland, Ireland, Australia, the United States, and in recent years, via Zoom, for online events that have reached thousands of participants from dozens of other countries on nearly every continent. The resonance of audiences to her voice, as mediated through my renditions, has been striking, particularly given the range of people gathered on such diverse occasions. As time went on and the accumulation of translated poems grew, the idea for this collection, *The Wandering Radiance*, came closer to realization.

From that point on, the work of completing this translation found support from a circle of friends whom I am delighted to thank. Alongside Gotthard's assistance with a handful of particularly slantwise passages in Domin's poems, my British friend and fellow poet Hilary Davies read an early draft of this book in its entirety, offering useful suggestions on various passages along the way. My deepest debt of gratitude is to my spouse, Rev. Dr. Ute Molitor, a native German speaker and a particularly adept reader and interpreter of poetry, which had something to do with how we met several decades ago. I am grateful for the creativity and insight she brought to working through puzzles posed by these poems. It was also a delight to talk through a number of such passages, musing together over how to render Domin's distinctive syntax and peculiar diction into English in ways that would cast something of the spell evoked by the original German. Beyond Ute's help with this book, I am also glad to thank her for the ways she embodies what Domin called "the postulate of the second chance: the new beginning." Her love has upheld that conviction in our lives when it was most needed, and she has always offered it with unswerving generosity, faithfulness, and courage.

I am also glad to acknowledge my debt of gratitude to Christopher Nelson of Green Linden Press whose commitment to publishing Domin's poems has been unwavering from the start. His support for the work of translation—and, as importantly, his encouragement of translators—embodies Edith Grossman's recognition that "the impact of the kind of artistic discovery that translation enables is profoundly important to the health and vitality of any language and any literature." From his early acceptance of several of these poems for publication in the journal *Under a Warm Green Linden* to his later commitment to publish *The Wandering Radiance*, his help and support have sustained the "artistic discovery" that brought this book to life. No translator could find a more impassioned champion of their work than Christopher has been.

Late in this journey, Marion Tauschwitz generously offered to write the Foreword for this volume. That she contributed her voice to this volume is a privilege and an honor, but also a distinct gain for readers for at least two reasons: first, because her work as the author of the definitive biography of Hilde Domin—*Hilde Domin. Dass ich sein kann, wie ich bin*—has deepened our understanding of the poet's life; and second, because her close personal friendship with Domin during the poet's later years lends her perspective an authenticity as a living witness. I am profoundly grateful that her remarks open *The Wandering Radiance*, alerting readers to Domin's importance within German culture and bringing them close to the inner spirit of her work.

The publication of this book comes on the centenary of my maternal grandparents' journey as immigrants to this country. To do so, they traveled by train from a town on the edge of the Black Forest, Schwenningen am Neckar, to Bremerhaven, and from there by steamer to Ellis Island before making their way, again by train, to Chicago where they began their lives anew. They were part of a wave of German immigration during the early 1920s to the United States, most drawn by the search for work and in the hope of making "a new beginning" here, to recall a theme so important to Domin. Their influence on my life and their generosity over the years have steeped me in the *mentalité* of this people as it lives through their language and culture—for, as Domin once put, we live "hand in hand with language to the last." My abiding thanks to them for their openness in sharing this heritage with me over the course of my life.

Finally, I am also glad to acknowledge a special debt of gratitude posthumously to Hilde Domin herself. Though we never met in life, I feel as though I have come to know her intimately through the companionship her writings—and above all her poems—has offered over the last fifteen years. Her commitment to writing "nevertheless-poems" (*Dennoch-Gedichte*) gives ample voice to her conviction that "the second chance" marks the true heart of what it means to be human. That assurance, with and through her poems, accompanied me through a particularly difficult period in my own life, in the early stages of this book's gestation. It is not too much to say that her voice, living through her poems, offered me *Heimat in der Sprache* and a deep sense of the *Geborgenheit* I desperately needed and desired—both through her words and on the strength of her courageous witness.

Only those who have faced the dislocation and absences of exile know, as Domin did, that "we cannot live without grace" (see "The Hardest Ways," 73). It is my hope that these poems will pass some sense of that grace along to other readers, "because the miracle is always happening." What I owe—what we all owe—Hilde Domin in times like ours is the commitment to live in solidarity with all who face Abel's fate in our world, so that we might live in answer to "the only question that matters": "Yes I am here" (in "Abel Get Up," 33). My hope is that the "*dennoch*–poems" collected here might inspire readers to join Domin in this witness. To be among those who refuse to turn away from others in their need. And, yes, to encourage and uphold those, like Abel, who need to hear this answer: "*Yes, we are here, we, your brother, we, your sister, we are here.*"

⁓

It is a pleasure to acknowledge S. Fischer Verlag for permission to publish my translation of Domin's essays ("Homeland and Exile") and to include the original German versions of the poems. These came, respectively, from the following sources: *Gesammelte Essays* (© S. Fischer Verlag GmbH, Frankfurt am Main 1993) and *Sämtliche Gedichte* (© S. Fischer Verlag GmbH, Frankfurt am Main 2009).

I am glad to acknowledge and thank the following journals in which these poems first appeared:

Bitter Oleander: "Easter Wind," "Exile"

Reunion: The Dallas Review: "Linguistics," "A Blue Day," "Easter Wind," "Escape from Here"

Under a Warm Green Linden: "Winter," "All My Ships," "Pulling Landscape," "Poetry"

3 CF SK

"Wandering Radiance" P.5

9

33

49

53

59 Cologne

77

79

147 chimes

283